Table of Contents

Letters to Parents ESL

Ready-to-Use Letters and Activities to Send Home in English and Spanish

Diane Pinkley

Teachers College
Columbia University

Good Year Books

An Imprint of Pearson Learning

Dedication

As always, to my children Gregoria, Jose, and Montserrat; to my wonderful grandson Adrian;
and to my sister Jennifer, who has shown unfailing love and support throughout.

 Good Year Books

are available for most basic curriculum subjects plus many enrichment areas. For more Good Year Books, contact your local
bookseller or educational dealer. For a complete catalog with information about other Good Year Books, please write:

Good Year Books
299 Jefferson Road
Parsippany, NJ 07054

Book and cover design: Rebidas Design Associates
Illustrations: Paul Somers
Spanish Adaptation: Patricia Abello

Editor: Susan Buntrock
Editorial Manager: Suzanne Beason
Executive Editor: Judith Adams
Publisher: Rosemary Calicchio

ISBN 0-673-59232-4

1 2 3 4 5 6 7 8 9 10 – PO – 05 04 03 02 01 00

Preface

The joys and satisfactions of teaching children from a variety of different cultures are many. However, the fact that these children and their families do have different languages, cultures, traditions, and expectations presents teachers with a number of challenges.

One of these challenges is the introduction of the idea that parental involvement is welcomed in American schools, and even expected to a certain degree. In many cultures, parental participation through consultation with a child's teachers, through a parent-teacher organization, or through shared activities at home is unknown. In fact, in some cultures, parents would never dream of approaching their child's teachers for any reason, as this would be considered a sign of disrespect or a sign that the teacher was not meeting the child's needs. It is therefore important to reinforce the idea of parental involvement and to point out what educators know to be true—that parents play a vital role in the cultural, social, emotional, and intellectual development of their children.

Letters to Parents: ESL is of particular value in encouraging parents of children studying English as a Second Language (ESL) to become involved in their children's educational development. Each letter is directed to ESL parents and contains a brief explanation of the importance of their participation, as well as simple activities focused on developing essential skills, which they may share with their children at home. These activities are designed to reinforce work done in the ESL classroom and address a wide variety of skills: listening, speaking, reading, writing, vocabulary, grammar, dictionary, critical thinking, and social/cultural development. In addition, they are not tied to any specific age group or grade level, though care was taken to include some activities appealing to younger children and others appealing to older children. All of them can be carried out at home with few materials and little preparation on the part of the parents. In short, *Letters to Parents: ESL* is ideal for the busy teacher who hopes to encourage parental involvement in their children's educational experience.

This book contains two versions of each letter—one in English and one in Spanish. Because the Spanish-speaking parents will be at various levels of English comprehension, it is recommended that they receive a copy of both versions to ensure clarity of understanding.

Diane Pinkley

How to Use This Book

Letters to Parents: ESL is designed to make your life as an ESL teacher easier by encouraging parental assistance with skills development on the part of your ESL students. Each of the activities suggested in the letters has been chosen to reinforce one or more of the following skill areas: listening, speaking, reading, writing, vocabulary, grammar, dictionary, critical thinking, and social/cultural development. Most of the activities require little or no preparation on the part of the parents, and all of them are designed to be interesting, challenging, and fun.

There is a total of thirty-seven letters: an Introductory Letter to the parents, and thirty-six Skills Development Letters, all of which are in English and Spanish. In addition, the book's Appendix will be very helpful to ESL students and to their parents because it contains information on basic spelling rules, pronunciation of English sounds, basic grammar terminology, and the principal parts of irregular verbs. This book also contains an evaluation form that you can send to parents from time to time during the school year to obtain feedback.

Recommended Procedure

1. At the beginning of the school year (or whenever a new ESL student joins the class), send home a copy of the Introductory Letter to the parents of each ESL child. If possible, copy the first letter onto official school stationery.

2. Each week (or almost each week) after that, send home one of the Skills Development Letters that reinforces the concepts you are working on in your classroom with your students. Send an evaluation form three to six times during the school year as well.

Preparation of the Letters

1. Photocopy one letter and sign your name at the bottom. Include the date at the top.

2. Make one copy of the letter for each student in your class and two additional copies for yourself. (Attach one copy to your weekly lesson plans and put the other in a binder, ready for students who lose their copy or for an arriving student.)

3. Send the letter home with your students on the same day of each week. (Wednesday or Thursday is good because parents then have time to plan when they will do some of the activities; they often choose the weekend.)

Helpful Tips

1. Encourage your students to get excited about working with their parents on the suggested activities. Emphasize that these activities are interesting and fun, not homework assignments. (In addition, observe family reactions to the idea. Some parents may ignore the letters completely; others may feel they cannot do them. If this happens, find out if the student has a sibling or aunt or other person who might be willing to participate. If no one is willing to work with the child, provide him or her with a simple Activity Fun book, of the type sold in supermarkets, or some other material that can be worked on independently. Encourage him or her to show you everything he or she is doing.)

2. Take advantage of the information about spelling rules, pronunciation, grammar terminology, and irregular verbs in the Appendix. Copy pages for students who need the information at hand, and make sure to copy this information for ESL parents whose English is either low-level or rusty.

3. If applicable, invite your students to bring in some of the projects they do at home for a "show and tell" session at some point during the school term.

4. If the majority of your students' parents seem receptive to participating in the activities, try scheduling a parent workshop once or twice during the year. Provide them with more ideas to use with their children, and get their comments and suggestions on how to improve their role in working with you and your school. Be sure to show your appreciation for their efforts.

Skill Charts

The Skills Development Letters in this book are not organized according to a fixed pattern or to an increasing level of complexity. You can therefore send home letters in any order, choosing activities that complement the material being studied in your textbook.

The Skill Summary Chart shows which particular skills and strategies are presented in each skill group. The Skills Distribution Chart is a quick way of seeing which activities focus on certain skills in that group's letters. Many of the activities address more than one skill at a time. The chart can be used, then, to individualize your letter selection. For example, you may want to make sure one child works on reading but at the same time also works on critical thinking skills. A look at the chart will show you which letters address those skills together. In this way, you can select activities most appropriate for individual students' needs.

Skill Summary Chart

Listening Letters distinguishing between sounds; distinguishing word endings; listening for details; listening for gist; listening for tone; intonation in questions; listening for similar meanings	**Speaking Letters** describing; giving opinions; giving commands/instructions; making suggestions; telling a story; reciting a poem/chant; pronouncing specific sounds	**Reading Letters** identifying the main idea/skimming; identifying details/scanning; predicting; making inferences; reading maps/graphics; analyzing
Writing Letters letter formation; describing; writing a letter; writing an ad; writing a story; writing notes; identifying topic sentences; identifying support sentences; writing an advice letter/column; paragraph organization	**Vocabulary Letters** labeling items; classifying words; matching words and definitions; guessing meaning from context; defining words; associating words; listing; memorizing words; relating forms of words	**Grammar Letters** grammar vocabulary; word order in sentences; subject-verb agreement; linking verbs with predicate adjectives; verb tenses; prepositions of place; pronoun reference; question formation; indefinite articles; gerunds and infinitives; possessive adjectives and pronouns; irregular plurals
Dictionary Letters scanning; associating; alternate spellings; parts of speech; using alphabetical order; guide words; homonyms; abbreviations; hyphenation; usage labels	**Critical Thinking Letters** associating; mnemonic devices; identifying cause and effect; making inferences; ranking; paraphrasing; using graphics; predicting; sequencing; comparing and contrasting; classifying	**Social/Cultural Letters** U.S. classroom expectations; recognizing and dealing with feelings; socially correct behavior choices; self-esteem; reading facial expressions and gestures; making a transition scrapbook; learning independence; using the public library; cultural sharing; fitting in; discussing values and ethics

Skills Distribution Chart

Skill	Letters
Listening	Listening letters 1–4; Speaking letters 1, 2, 4; Reading letter 3; Writing letters 1, 3; Vocabulary letters 1–4; Grammar letters 2, 3; Critical Thinking letters 2, 4; Social/Cultural letters 1–4
Speaking	Speaking letters 1–4; Listening letters 2, 3; Reading letters 1, 3, 4; Writing letters 1, 2 4; Vocabulary letters 1, 3, 4; Grammar letters 1–4; Dictionary letter 2; Critical Thinking letters 1, 2, 3; Social/Cultural Letters 1–4
Reading	Reading letters 1–4; Speaking letters 1, 4; Vocabulary letters 1, 2, 3; Grammar letter 3; Dictionary letter 3; Critical Thinking letters 1, 2, 4; Social/Cultural letters 3, 4
Writing	Writing letters 1–4; Reading letter 3; Vocabulary letters 1, 2, 4; Grammar letter 4; Critical Thinking letters 1, 3; Social/Cultural letters 3, 4
Vocabulary	Vocabulary letters 1–4; Listening letters 2, 3; Speaking letters 1–4; Grammar letter 4; Dictionary letter 2; Critical Thinking letters 3, 4; Social/Cultural letter 1
Grammar	Grammar letters 1–4; Listening letters 1, 2, 4; Writing letter 2; Dictionary letter 2
Dictionary	Dictionary letters 1–4; Speaking letters 1, 4; Reading letters 1, 4; Writing letters 2, 4; Vocabulary letter 4; Critical Thinking letter 3
Critical Thinking	Critical Thinking letters 1–4; Listening letters 1, 4; Speaking letter 1; Reading letters 2, 3, 4; Writing letters 3, 4; Vocabulary letters 1–4; Grammar letters 1, 2, 4; Dictionary letters 1, 2; Social/Cultural letters 1, 2
Social/Cultural	Social/Cultural letters 1–4; Listening letter 2; Speaking letters 1, 2, 4; Reading letters 3, 4; Writing letters 2, 4; Vocabulary letter 4

Evaluation Form

Dear Parents:

By now you have received a number of ESL Skills Development Letters listing activities to share with your child at home. These suggested activities are meant to provide your child with additional practice in the skills so important to successful language learning.

As your child's ESL teacher, I would very much appreciate hearing your reaction to these reinforcement activities. Your comments and suggestions will help me better serve your child and his or her classmates. Please take a minute or two to complete the evaluation below. Have your child return this form to me at school. Thank you for your interest and participation.

Please mark the correct column with a check (✓).

My child and I found the skills development activities to be:

Skill Activities	Excellent	Good	Average	Not Useful
Listening				
Speaking				
Reading				
Writing				
Vocabulary				
Grammar				
Dictionary				
Critical Thinking				
Social/Cultural				

Your Comments:

_____   _____

Signature of Parent or Guardian   Date

Cuestionario de evaluación

Estimados padres de familia:

Hasta la fecha han recibido una serie de cartas para el "Fomento de Destrezas del Inglés como Segundo Idioma" (ESL), donde aparecen varias actividades que puede realizar con su hijo o hija. Estas sugerencias tienen como fin permitirle a su hijo/a que practique en casa las destrezas básicas para aprender un idioma.

Como maestro(a) de su hijo/a de Inglés como Segundo Idioma (ESL), me gustaría conocer su opinión sobre esas actividades de refuerzo. Sus comentarios y sugerencias me ayudarán a servirle mejor a su hijo/a y a sus compañeros de clase. Por favor dedique un rato a contestar la siguiente evaluación y envíela con su hijo/a a la escuela. Agradezco su interés y participación.

Por favor, señale la columna correcta con una marca (✔).

Mi hijo/a y yo consideramos que las actividades para el fomento de destrezas son:

Tipo de actividad	Excelente	Buena	Regular	No es Útil
Habilidad de escuchar				
Conversación				
Lectura				
Escritura				
Vocabulario				
Gramática				
Uso del diccionario				
Pensamiento crítico				
Desarrollo socio/cultural				

Comentarios:

_____   _____

Firma del padre o guardián: Fecha

Introductory Letter

Dear Parents,

As parents, you want the best life possible for your child. One of the most important ways you can contribute to your child's success in life is through the development of shared learning experiences that take place with the family at home. You are in a unique position to help your child achieve academic and social success through your interest, patience, and support. Because you are parents, your child already sees you as a guide and teacher in many areas, and you already play key roles in his or her growth and development. By working together, I believe that we will contribute in an important way to your child's potential for academic and social success in school and in later life.

During this school year, your child will be studying English as a Second Language along with many other subjects such as history and science. In learning English, your child will work on many different skill areas necessary for successful communication. These areas include: listening, speaking, dictionary, reading, writing, vocabulary, grammar, critical thinking, and social/cultural development. In order to help reinforce the classroom work in these areas, I will be sending to your home prepared letters that will provide you with useful, pleasurable ideas and activities to share with your child. Working together on these activities at home will strengthen your child's learning potential and increase his or her chances for success in the classroom. Please note that these ideas and activities are structured so that they do not require a great deal of your time or expensive materials and equipment. Your main contribution will be your interest, support, and satisfaction as you make an active difference in your child's potential success both in the classroom and beyond.

I look forward to working together with you this year to provide your child with the very best of educational opportunities in school and at home. Your participation and interest are valued, so please feel free to contact me with any questions or ideas that you may have. Your child is worth it!

Sincerely,

Carta de introducción

Estimados padres de familia:

Todo padre desea lo mejor para sus hijos. Una de las mejores formas de contribuir a que su hijo o hija tenga éxito en la vida es compartir en el hogar experiencias que fomenten el aprendizaje. Ustedes tienen en sus manos la oportunidad de ayudar a su hijo/a a alcanzar el éxito académico y social mediante su interés, su paciencia y su apoyo. Como padres, ustedes ya son guías y maestros de su hijo/a en muchas áreas. Ya desempeñan un importante papel en su crecimiento y desarrollo. Al trabajar juntos, considero que haremos una importante contribución al potencial de su hijo/a para que alcance el éxito académico y social tanto en la escuela como en su vida futura.

Durante este año escolar, su hijo/a estudiará Inglés como Segundo Idioma conjuntamente con muchas otras materias tales como historia y ciencias. Al aprender inglés, su hijo/a practicará diversas destrezas necesarias para una comunicación efectiva. Estas áreas incluyen habilidad de escuchar, conversación, uso del diccionario, lectura, escritura, vocabulario, gramática, pensamiento crítico y desarrollo socio/cultural. Con el fin de ayudar a reforzar el trabajo que hacemos en el salón de clase en estas áreas, les enviaré a la casa unas cartas con útiles y placenteras sugerencias y actividades para que realicen con su hijo/a. El llevar a cabo estas actividades en el hogar fomentará el potencial de aprendizaje de su hijo/a e incrementará su oportunidad de éxito en el salón de clase. Puesto que estas ideas y actividades están estructuradas, no exigirán mucho tiempo de su parte ni materiales o equipos costosos. Su principal contribución será su interés, su apoyo y la satisfacción de saber que está fomentando el éxito potencial de su hijo/a en el salón de clase y más allá del mismo.

Me complacerá trabajar con usted este año para darle a su hijo/a las mejores oportunidades educativas tanto en la escuela como en la casa. Su participación e interés es muy apreciado, así que no duden en comunicarse conmigo si tienen cualquier pregunta o idea. ¡Su hijo/a se lo merece!

Atentamente,

Dear Parents,

Listening is very important in learning a language. Some listening skills are related to pronunciation, such as distinguishing word endings and intonation. Others are related to understanding the meaning of what we hear in the new language, such as distinguishing the main idea or important details. As parents, you can help your child develop better listening skills that are so essential to success in the classroom.

1. Rhyme Time. Call out four or five words, one of which does not rhyme. Have your child tell you which word does not have the same sound as the other words. For example, repeat *sky, eye, pie, pen,* and *fly.* Your child should tell you that *pen* sounds different from the other words. Repeat using many groups of rhyming words with different sounds.

2. One or Many? To help your child distinguish word endings such as those that show singular and plural, call out groups of related words, changing at random from singular to plural. For example, use words for fruit, such as *banana/bananas, orange/oranges, pear/pears, grape/grapes,* and so on. Have your child say *one* or *many,* depending on the word ending used.

3. Where Am I? Help your child listen for important details. Tell him or her that you will describe a place and that he or she will have to listen carefully and then tell you what kind of place you are describing. For example, you may say something like the following: "Walking down the street, I see a place that I go into. There are several people here. Two are waiting in chairs and reading magazines. One is looking at himself in a hand mirror. A man is sitting in a special chair while another man is putting white, foamy soap on his face. Then he takes a razor and begins to shave the man's face. At another chair, a man is cutting a little boy's hair. Where am I?" (At a barbershop).

NOTE: If you or other family members speak English, do the activities in English with your child. If you do not, do them in your own language, and they will still help your child focus on strategies that will eventually transfer to better listening comprehension in English.

Estimados padres de familia:

En el aprendizaje de un idioma es muy importante la habilidad de escuchar. Parte de esa habilidad está relacionada con la pronunciación, como el saber distinguir la terminación de las palabras y la entonación. También está relacionada con la comprensión de lo que escuchamos en el nuevo idioma, tal como distinguir la idea principal o los detalles importantes. Como padres, ustedes pueden ayudarle a su hijo o hija a desarrollar la habilidad de escuchar que es esencial para el éxito en el salón de clase.

1. A rimar se dijo. Mencione cuatro o cinco palabras, una de las cuales no rime. Pídale a su hijo/a que le diga qué palabra no tiene el mismo sonido de las demás palabras. Por ejemplo, repita las palabras *miel, piel, fiel, cielo* y *cruel.* Su hijo/a debe decirle que *cielo* suena diferente a las demás palabras. Repita la actividad con varios grupos de palabras que rimen con diferentes sonidos.

2. ¿Uno o varios? Para ayudar a su hijo/a a distinguir terminaciones de palabras como las que indican singular y plural, mencione grupos de palabras relacionadas, cambiando al azar de singular a plural. Por ejemplo, diga nombres de frutas, como *banana/bananas, naranja/naranjas, pera/peras, uva/uvas* y así sucesivamente. Pida a su hijo/a que diga *uno* o *varios,* dependiendo de la terminación usada.

3. ¿Dónde estoy? Ayude a su hijo/a a aprender a escuchar detalles importantes. Usted describirá un lugar. Pídale que oiga con atención y que después le diga qué tipo de lugar usted está describiendo. Por ejemplo, usted podría decir: "Camino por la calle y veo un lugar al que entro. Allí hay varios hombres. Dos esperan sentados leyendo revistas. Otro se está mirando en un espejo de mano. Un señor está sentado en una silla especial mientras que otro le pone una espuma blanca en la cara. Después empieza a afeitarlo con una rasuradora. En otra silla, un hombre le corta el pelo a un niño. ¿Dónde estoy?" (En una barbería).

NOTA: Si usted u otro miembro de la familia habla inglés, realice las actividades con su hijo/a en inglés. Si no sabe inglés, hágalas en su propio idioma porque de cualquier forma le ayudarán a su hijo/a a fomentar estrategias que le permitirán mejorar su habilidad para escuchar y comprender en inglés.

Dear Parents,

As parents, you want your child to succeed in learning English. One way you can help is to provide practice with developing the skills necessary to achieve academic success. Listening is a particularly important skill in language learning. You can help your child focus on important differences in sounds, rhythm, and intonation. You can also help him or her listen for the main idea or for key details in a text.

1. True/False. To help your child distinguish between word endings, make sentences using *can* and *can't*. Have your child tell you if your statement is true or false. For example, if you say, "People can't fly but birds can," your child would say, "True."

2. Right Response. Write the following responses on separate slips of paper: Thank you./Excuse me./I don't know./That's a great idea./I'm sorry. Have your child hold up the appropriate response (or repeat it) for each of several different sentences you make, such as: You look very pretty today./You stepped on my foot./Where is our neighbor?/Let's go to the park./I lost my dog.

3. Questions. To help your child identify the intonation patterns used in questions in English, repeat a number of mixed statements and questions. Have your child identify the questions by saying "question" each time you ask a question. For example, you may say, "The sun is shining today./It's dinner time./What time is it?/Are you happy?/It's late." Your child will say "question" after the third and fourth sentences.

4. TV Commercial Blackout. When a commercial comes on, darken your TV screen to black but leave on the sound. Ask your child to give you the main idea of what the people are talking about. You can check his or her answer by looking at the commercial together the next time it is shown. This activity works well with the radio too.

NOTE: If you or other family members speak English, do the activities in English with your child. If you do not, do them in your own language, and they will still help your child focus on strategies that will eventually transfer to better listening comprehension in English.

13

Estimados padres de familia:

Como padres, ustedes desean que su hijo o hija aprenda bien inglés. Un modo de ayudarle es dándole la oportunidad de practicar las destrezas necesarias para alcanzar el éxito académico. El escuchar es una destreza particularmente importante en el aprendizaje de un idioma. Ustedes pueden ayudarle a su hijo/a a concentrarse en las diferencias importantes de sonidos, ritmos y entonación. También pueden ayudarle a escuchar la idea principal o los detalles claves de un texto.

1. Verdadero o falso. Para ayudar a su hijo/a a distinguir las terminaciones de palabras, haga oraciones usando las palabras can y can't. Pídale a su hijo/a que diga si su declaración es verdadera o falsa. Por ejemplo, si usted dice: "La gente no puede volar pero los pájaros sí pueden. ("People can't fly but birds can), su hijo/a debe decir "verdadero".

2. Respuesta apropiada. Escriba las siguientes respuestas en tiras de papel aparte: "Gracias/ Discúlpame/ No sé./ ¡Qué buena idea!/ Lo siento mucho". Pida a su hijo/a que muestre la respuesta apropiada (o que la repita) cada vez que usted diga una oración, tal como "Estás muy linda hoy./ Me pisaste./ ¿Dónde está nuestro vecino?/Vamos al parque/. Se me perdió mi perro".

3. Preguntas. Para ayudar a su hijo/a a identificar los patrones de entonación que se usan en las preguntas en inglés, repita varias afirmaciones y preguntas mezcladas. Pida a su hijo/a que diga "pregunta" cada vez que escuche una pregunta. Por ejemplo, usted podría decir: "El sol brilla hoy./Es hora de comer./¿Qué hora es?/¿Estás contento?/Es muy tarde." Su hijo/a dirá "pregunta" después de oír la tercera y la cuarta oración.

4. Pantalla en negro. Cuando se transmita un comercial por televisión, oscurezca la pantalla del televisor pero deje el sonido. Pídale a su hijo/a que diga la idea principal de la conversación que escucha. Para verificar su respuesta, pueden mirar el comercial juntos la próxima vez que se transmita. Esta actividad también es muy apropiada con comerciales de radio.

NOTA: Si usted u otro miembro de la familia habla inglés, realice las actividades con su hijo/a en inglés. Si no sabe inglés, hágalas en su propio idioma porque de cualquier forma le ayudarán a su hijo/a a fomentar estrategias que le permitirán mejorar su habilidad para escuchar y comprender en inglés.

Dear Parents,

Speaking English requires the development of good listening skills. It is important for your child to practice listening for main ideas and for details, as well as to practice recognizing words and discriminating sounds. You can help your child learn English more efficiently by providing additional practice with listening. Expose your child to as much spoken English as possible (TV, radio, films, etc.) and encourage him or her to share in the activities below.

1. Memory Chain. To help your child listen for key words, begin by saying, "I'm going on vacation and I'm taking a camera." Your child must listen and then repeat the whole sentence, adding one more item, for example, "I'm going on vacation and I'm taking a camera and film." You then repeat that whole sentence and add on another item. "I'm going on vacation and I'm taking a camera and film and a swimsuit." Then it is his or her turn again, and so on.

2. Bingo. To practice sound discrimination, give your child Bingo cards with numbers and markers. Call out a prepared list of numbers in English, and award a prize when he or she has correctly marked all the numbers on the Bingo card. (It is especially helpful to contrast the pronunciation of 13 and 30, 14 and 40, 15 and 50, 16 and 60, 17 and 70, 18 and 80, and 19 and 90.) This game is really fun when there are several players.

3. Radio Songs. Listen to a song in English on the radio together with your child. Ask him or her to identify the main idea of the song from a list of possibilities you provide. You could also have two or three possible titles on a sheet of paper and ask him or her to choose the best title for the song based on his or her understanding of the lyrics.

NOTE: If you or other family members speak English, do the activities in English with your child. If you do not, do them in your own language, and they will still help your child focus on strategies that will eventually transfer to better listening comprehension in English.

Estimados padres de familia:

Para hablar en inglés se necesita desarrollar bien la habilidad de escuchar. Es importante que su hijo o hija practique la habilidad de captar ideas principales y detalles, así como el reconocimiento de palabras y la diferenciación de sonidos. Usted puede ayudarle a aprender inglés más efectivamente dándole oportunidades adicionales de que escuche inglés. Exponga a su hijo/a al inglés verbal lo más que sea posible (televisión, radio, cine, etc.) e invítelo a hacer con usted las siguientes actividades.

1. En cadena. Para ayudar a su hijo/a a escuchar palabras claves, comience por decir: "Me voy de vacaciones y llevo mi cámara". Después de escuchar, su hijo/a debe repetir la oración completa, añadiendo más información. Por ejemplo: "Me voy de vacaciones y llevo mi cámara y rollo de fotos". Entonces usted repite esa oración completa y agrega otro objeto. "Me voy de vacaciones y llevo mi cámara, rollo de fotos y un traje de baño". Después es el turno de su hijo/a y así sucesivamente.

2. Bingo. Para que practique la diferenciación de sonidos, dele a su hijo/a marcadores y un cartón de Bingo con números. Lea una lista de números en inglés escritos previamente, y dele un premio a su hijo/a cuando haya marcado correctamente todos esos números en el cartón de Bingo. (Es particularmente útil hacer un contraste en la pronunciación en inglés entre 13 y 30, 14 y 40, 15 y 50, 16 y 60, 17 y 70, 18 y 80 y 19 y 90.) Este juego es muy divertido con varias personas.

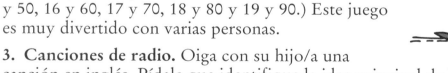

3. Canciones de radio. Oiga con su hijo/a una canción en inglés. Pídale que identifique la idea principal de la canción entre una lista de posibilidades que usted le da. También podría escribir dos o tres títulos posibles en una hoja de papel y pedirle que escoja el mejor título para la canción basándose en lo que captó de la letra de la canción.

NOTA: Si usted u otro miembro de la familia habla inglés, realice las actividades con su hijo/a en inglés. Si no sabe inglés, hágalas en su propio idioma porque de cualquier forma le ayudarán a su hijo/a a fomentar estrategias que le permitirán mejorar su habilidad para escuchar y comprender en inglés.

Dear Parents,

Success in the classroom depends on many skills, among them the very important skill of listening. When we look at listening in relation to learning a language, we focus on listening for the main idea, for important details, for associations, or for tone. It is also very important to practice distinguishing between sounds, recognizing grammatical cues, and recognizing words. You can help your child by sharing the activities below.

1. Past, Present, Future. To help your child focus on grammatical cues such as verb tense, repeat a number of sentences using the present, past, and future tenses. Have your child say, "past," "present," or "future" after each sentence. For example, you may say, "I watched three programs on TV./I'll go to the store later./I'm having fun with you." Your child will say, "past," "future," and "present."

2. Tone. Help your child become aware of the emotional content of language by repeating the same sentence in a variety of ways. Have him or her identify the tone of your statement each time. For example, you may repeat the sentence, "The mail isn't here yet," the first time with a neutral tone, then with an angry tone, then with a worried tone, then with a disappointed tone, then with a sarcastic tone, then with an incredulous tone, and so on.

"The mail isn't here yet."

3. Same or Different? Prepare several pairs of sentences, some of which mean the same and some of which have different meanings. Have your child tell you which pairs are similar and which pairs are different in meaning. For example, you may say, "I'm crazy about chocolate./I really love chocolate."(same meaning) or "They made up after the argument./They made up a story." (different meanings), and so on.

NOTE: If you or other family members speak English, do the activities in English with your child. If you do not, do them in your own language, and they will still help your child focus on strategies that will eventually transfer to better listening comprehension in English.

Estimados padres de familia:

El éxito en el salón de clase depende de mucha destrezas, entre ellas la importante habilidad de escuchar. Cuando hablamos de escuchar en relación con el aprendizaje de un idioma, nos concentramos en prestar atención a la idea principal, los detalles importantes, las asociaciones o el tono. También es muy importante practicar la distinción de sonidos, reconocer pautas gramaticales y distinguir palabras. Para ayudar a su hijo/a, pueden realizar las siguientes actividades.

1. Pasado, presente, futuro. Para ayudar a su hijo/a a enfocarse en pautas gramaticales tales como el tiempo del verbo, repita una serie de oraciones usando los tiempos presente, pasado y futuro. Pida a su hijo/a que diga "pasado", "presente" o "futuro" después de cada oración. Por ejemplo, usted podría decir: "Vi tres programas de televisión./Más tardé iré al supermercado./Me estoy divirtiendo contigo."
Su hijo/a dirá "pasado", "futuro" y "presente".

2. Tono. Ayude a su hijo/a a captar el contenido emocional del lenguaje repitiendo la misma oración de varias formas. Pídale que identifique el tono de lo que usted diga cada vez. Por ejemplo, usted puede repetir la oración "Aún no ha llegado el correo", la primera vez con un tono neutral, luego con un tono enfadado, luego con un tono de preocupación, luego con un tono de desilusión, luego con un tono sarcástico, luego con un tono incrédulo y así sucesivamente.

¡Todavía no ha llegado el correo!

3. ¿Igual o diferente? Prepare varios pares de oraciones, algunas con el mismo significado y algunos con diferente significado. Pídale a su hijo/a que diga qué pares son similares y qué pares son diferentes en significado. Por ejemplo, usted podría decir "Me gustan mucho los chocolates"./Me encantan los chocolates". (mismo significado) o "Tómate la sopa/La sopa es de tomate" (diferente significado), y así sucesivamente.

NOTA: Si usted u otro miembro de la familia habla inglés, realice las actividades con su hijo/a en inglés. Si no sabe inglés, hágalas en su propio idioma porque de cualquier forma le ayudarán a su hijo/a a fomentar estrategias que le permitirán mejorar su habilidad para escuchar y comprender en inglés.

Dear Parents,

Children learn their first language surrounded by their families at home. Just as you played an important role in helping your child with speaking his or her first language, you can help your child with speaking English through sharing some simple activities at home. Some of the activities below focus on meaningful communication. Others focus on pronunciation of English.

1. English Time. Set aside a few minutes each day to practice English. It may be in the car, during breakfast, or at bedtime. During that time, encourage your child to describe what he or she learned in class that day and then practice the new language. For example, if your child learned the language of expressing opinions, give your own opinion of a TV show, a movie, a popular singer, a sports figure, and so on. Have your child then give his or her own opinion in English.

2. Robot. Pretend that you are a robot and cannot do anything unless your child gives you instructions in English. For example, have your child tell you how to set the dinner table or fold laundry or make a snack to eat. If new words are needed, provide an English dictionary for your child to use.

3. Puppets. Make simple puppets from small paper bags or old socks. Allow your child to decorate them and name them. Then use the puppets to practice short conversations in English about typical situations. For example, one puppet may feel sick or have a headache. The other puppet can provide suggestions about staying in bed, taking medicine, calling the doctor, and so on.

4. Chants and Poems. To help your child increase awareness of stress, rhythm, and intonation patterns in English, choose a popular nursery rhyme, chant, or short poem to have your child memorize and perform for the family. Make a collection or a tape to keep of the pieces he or she learns.

NOTE: If you or other family members speak English, do the activities in English with your child. If you do not, do your part of the activities in your own language and have your child respond to you in English.

Estimados padres de familia:

Los niños aprenden su primer idioma dentro del ambiente hogareño. Así como ustedes ayudaron de modo fundamental a que su hijo o hija hablara su primer idioma, también pueden ayudarle a hablar inglés realizando juntos unas sencillas actividades en casa. Algunas actividades se centran en la comunicación efectiva y otras en la pronunciación del inglés.

1. Sólo en inglés. Dedique unos cuantos minutos al día a practicar inglés. Puede ser en el auto, a la hora del desayuno o antes de acostarse. Durante ese momento, anime a su hijo/a describir lo que aprendió en la clase ese día y después pídale que practique el nuevo lenguaje. Por ejemplo, si aprendió el lenguaje para expresar opiniones, dé su propia opinión sobre un programa de televisión, una película, un cantante popular, un deportista o algo por el estilo. Entonces pida a su hijo/a que dé su propia opinión en inglés.

2. Robot. Imagine que usted es un robot que sólo sigue las instrucciones que su hijo/a le da en inglés. Por ejemplo, pídale a su hijo/a que le diga cómo poner la mesa, doblar la ropa lavada o preparar algo de comer. Si su hijo/a necesita más palabras, puede usar un diccionario.

3. Títeres. Elabore unos títeres sencillos con bolsas pequeñas de papel o calcetines viejos. Invite a su hijo/a a decorarlos y ponerles nombres. Después use los títeres para practicar conversaciones cortas en inglés acerca de situaciones corrientes. Por ejemplo, un títere puede sentirse mal o tener dolor de cabeza. El otro títere puede sugerirle que se quede acostado, que tome un remedio, que llame al doctor, y así sucesivamente.

4. Rimas y poemas. Para ayudar a su hijo/a a hacerse más consciente del énfasis, el ritmo y de los patrones de entonación en inglés, elija una canción de cuna popular, una rima o un poema corto para que su hijo/a lo memorice y lo represente frente a la familia. Como recuerdo, haga una colección de las piezas o grabe a su hijo/a mientras las entona.

NOTA: Si usted u otro miembro de la familia habla inglés, realice las actividades con su hijo/a en inglés. Si no sabe inglés, haga la parte que le corresponde en su propio idioma y pídale a su hijo que le responda en inglés.

Dear Parents,

Your child is learning all about English at school, and you can play an important role in helping him or her to make progress in speaking English at home. The more opportunities your child has to speak English outside of the classroom, the more he or she will improve. (Children from six to twelve learn especially quickly because they are less self-conscious about the possibility of making mistakes.) Encourage your child as much as you can.

1. Mystery Box. Put three to five different items in a box. Have your child close his or her eyes and feel one of the items. Have him or her describe it in English without looking at it. Repeat with the other items. You may want to take turns feeling and describing the mystery objects.

2. Picture Stories. Cut out a variety of pictures from magazines, newspapers, postcards, and so on. Put them in a paper bag. Pull out a picture and start a story based on that picture. Then, after a sentence or two, have your child pull out another picture and continue the same story, incorporating new details based on his or her picture. Take turns pulling out pictures and telling the story until you use up all the pictures or end the story at a logical place. This activity is fun to play with several family members too.

3. What Am I Doing? Mime an action such as swimming or typing a letter and have your child guess the activity, describing in English what you are doing. Take turns performing and guessing a variety of actions.

4. Mini-situations. On separate slips of paper, write situations such as "at the doctor's office, at the gas station, at the movies, at the airport," and so on. Put them in a pile on the table and choose one of the situations. Begin a conversation that would typically take place in that situation and have your child continue. Take turns choosing the slips of paper until they are all used. For example, if you chose "at the grocery store," you could begin by saying, "Excuse me, are these apples on sale today?" Your child would continue, saying, "No, Ma'am. Pears are on sale today."

NOTE: If you or other family members speak English, do the activities in English with your child. If you do not, do your part of the activities in your own language and have your child respond to you in English.

Estimados padres de familia:

Su hijo/a está aprendiendo en la escuela todo lo relativo al inglés. Ustedes pueden desempeñar un importante papel para ayudarle en la casa a mejorar su conversación en inglés. Cuantas más oportunidades tenga su hijo/a de hablar inglés fuera del salón de clase, mayores serán sus progresos. (Los niños de seis a doce años aprenden especialmente rápido porque son menos conscientes de la posibilidad de cometer errores.) Anime a su hijo/a todo lo que más pueda.

1. La caja misteriosa. Coloque de tres a cinco objetos diferentes en una caja. Pida a su hijo/a que cierre los ojos y que palpe uno de los objetos. Pídale que lo describa en inglés sin mirarlo. Repita la actividad con otros objetos. Pueden turnarse para palpar y describir los objetos misteriosos.

2. Cuentos ilustrados. Recorte diversas ilustraciones de revistas, periódicos, tarjetas postales, etc. Póngalas en una bolsa de papel. Saque una ilustración e inicie un cuento basándose en esa ilustración. Después dé una o dos oraciones, pida a su hijo/a que saque otra ilustración y que continúe el mismo cuento, incorporando nuevos detalles basados en su ilustración. Túrnense para sacar ilustraciones y continuar el cuento hasta que usen todas las ilustraciones o hasta que el cuento termine de modo lógico. Esta actividad también es divertida con otros miembros de la familia.

3. ¿Qué estoy haciendo? Represente una acción tal como nadar o escribir una carta a máquina, y pida a su hijo/a que adivine la actividad, describiendo en inglés lo que usted está haciendo. Túrnense para representar y adivinar diversas acciones.

4. Mini-situaciones. En tiras de papel aparte, escriba situaciones tales como "en el consultorio del doctor, en la estación de gasolina, en el cine, en el aeropuerto" y así sucesivamente. Póngalas en un montón sobre una mesa y elija una de las situaciones. Comience una conversación que podría tener lugar en dicha situación y pida a su hijo/a que la continúe. Túrnense para sacar tiras de papel hasta usarlas todas. Por ejemplo, si saca una tira que diga "en el supermercado", podría iniciar la conversación diciendo "Perdón. ¿Podría decirme si las manzanas están rebajadas hoy?" Su hijo/a continuaría diciendo: "No señora. Pero las peras sí están rebajadas".

NOTA: Si usted u otro miembro de la familia habla inglés, realice las actividades con su hijo/a en inglés. Si no sabe inglés, haga la parte que le corresponde en su propio idioma y pídale a su hijo que le responda en inglés.

Dear Parents,

Learning to speak a second language takes practice. Your child should take advantage of every opportunity to increase fluency and accuracy. As parents, you can encourage your child to speak more English by sharing the activities mentioned below. Some of them deal with aspects of pronunciation of English; others deal with meaningful communication.

1. Tongue Twisters. To help your child master the pronunciation of certain sounds, have fun with tongue twisters. Challenge your child to see who can say each one quickly without making a mistake. Some common ones are "She sells seashells down by the seashore, Peter Piper picked a peck of pickled peppers, Duchess Diana daintily downed her dinner, Rubber baby buggy bumpers," and "Betty bought some bitter butter." Have your child make up examples too.

2. Drawing Dictation. Have your child draw a simple picture. Then, have him or her tell you exactly how to duplicate his or her picture by giving you step-by-step instructions. You cannot see his or her picture until you have finished your drawing. It's fun to compare how closely your picture matches that of your child. Discuss how clear the instructions were and how they could be rephrased for more clarity.

3. Minute Speeches. Prepare a number of slips of paper, each of which has a word or words such as *apples, baseball, girls, motorcycles, cartoons, favorite toy,* and *money.* Put them in an envelope and have your child draw a slip of paper, talking about that subject for one full minute without stopping. A timer comes in handy for this activity.

4. Picture Perfect. Prepare several photos or pictures of fairly complex scenes. Have your child choose one and study it closely for one minute. Then take away the picture and have him or her describe everything he or she can remember that is in the picture.

NOTE: If you or other family members speak English, do the activities in English with your child. If you do not, do your part of the activities in your own language and have your child respond to you in English.

Estimados padres de familia:

Para aprender a hablar un segundo idioma hay que practicarlo. Su hijo/a debe aprovechar cualquier oportunidad de aumentar su fluidez y precisión. Como padres, ustedes pueden estimularlo a que hable más inglés realizando juntos las actividades que se describen a continuación. Algunas giran en torno a la pronunciación en inglés; otras se enfocan en una comunicación efectiva.

1. Trabalenguas. Para ayudar a su hijo/a a dominar la pronunciación de ciertos sonidos, diviértanse con trabalenguas. Desafíe a su hijo/a a ver quién puede decir cada trabalenguas rápidamente sin equivocarse. Un trabalenguas muy conocido en español es: "Tres tristes tigres comían en tres tristes platos de trigo" (Vea los trabalenguas que se sugieren en inglés). Anime a su hijo/a a que invente sus propios trabalenguas.

2. Díctame tu dibujo. Pida a su hijo/a que haga un dibujo sencillo. Después, pídale que le diga cómo duplicar exactamente el dibujo dándole instrucciones paso por paso. Usted no puede ver el dibujo de su hijo/a mientras lo duplica. Cuando termine, será divertido ver si los dos dibujos se parecen. Comenten si las instrucciones fueron claras y como se podrían mejorar.

3. Dicursos de un minuto.
Escriba en tiras de papel aparte una serie de palabras o conceptos como *manzanas, béisbol, niñas, motocicletas, tiras cómicas, tu juguete favorito* y *dinero*. Póngalas dentro de un sobre y pida a su hijo/a que saque una tira de papel. Anímelo/a que hable de ese tema durante un minuto sin parar. En esta actividad puede ser muy útil un cronómetro.

4. Describe la escena. Prepare varias fotos o ilustraciones que muestren escenas relativamente complejas. Pida a su hijo/a que elija una y que la observe de cerca por un minuto. Después retire la ilustración y pídale que describa todo lo que recuerde de la misma.

NOTA: Si usted u otro miembro de la familia habla inglés, realice las actividades con su hijo/a en inglés. Si no sabe inglés, haga la parte que le corresponde en su propio idioma y pídale a su hijo que le responda en inglés.

Dear Parents,

Encouraging your child to take advantage of opportunities to speak English outside the classroom can be of great help. You can help him or her improve in pronunciation, accuracy, and fluency through sharing a few simple activities. Make sure your child is exposed to spoken English through TV, radio, movies, and music, because listening and speaking are closely connected.

1. Commercial Break. Have your child listen to a few TV commercials in English as preparation. Then, give him or her a choice of common items around the house to make a commercial about. For example, your child might do a commercial about a laundry detergent, cereal, pair of jeans, sports shoe, perfume, and so on. Help him or her with props such as music, objects, and so forth. If possible, tape your child's commercials to enjoy later.

2. Biographies. This is a fun game to do in the car or at the table. Choose letters and sounds that your child needs practice with, and then have him or her make up crazy biographies, each of which uses the letter or sound as much as possible. As an example, say, "Alice Arby lives in Athens at 22 Arbuckle Street. Alice is in the army. She works in the armory where she adds up arms. Alice adores her pet armadillo, apples, and absolutely awful jokes." Sound combinations that are useful to practice include /b/ and /v/, /v/ and /w/, and /l/ and /r/.

3. Comic Book Summaries. After your child has finished one of his or her favorite comics, have him or her tell you what the story was about in simple English. You can do the same with cartoons on TV.

4. All You Know. Get in the habit of reading the newspaper and commenting on some of the more important news stories with your child. At the end of the week, name one of the major news items and have him or her tell you all he or she knows about the subject in English.

NOTE: If you or other family members speak English, do the activities in English with your child. If you do not, do your part of the activities in your own language and have your child respond to you in English.

Estimados padres de familia:

El estimular a su hijo o hija a que hable inglés fuera del salón de clase es muy favorable. Para ayudarle a mejorar la pronunciación, así como la precisión y la fluidez verbal, puede realizar unas actividades muy sencillas. Asegúrese de que su hijo/a esté en contacto con el inglés oral a través de la televisión, la radio, el cine y la música, puesto que el escuchar y el hablar están muy vinculados.

1. Comerciales. Como preparativo, pida a su hijo/a que escuche unos cuantos comerciales de televisión en inglés. Después, anímelo a que escoja algún artículo doméstico para promocionar. Por ejemplo, su hijo/a podría hacer un comercial acerca de detergentes de ropa, cereales, jeans, zapatos deportivos, perfumes, y así

sucesivamente. Ayúdele a buscar la música y los objetos necesarios para su comercial. Si es posible, grabe los comerciales de su hijo/a para que puedan disfrutarlos más adelante.

2. Biografías. Éste es un juego muy divertido para el auto o en la mesa de comer. Elija letras y sonidos que su hijo/a necesite practicar y después pídale que invente biografías cómicas, usando esa letra o ese sonido lo más posible. Un ejemplo podría ser: "Alicia Alvarez vive en Atlanta, en la calle Argaez. Alicia está en la armada y trabaja en el almacén de armas. Alicia adora a su armadillo y le encantan las almendras y las adivinanzas". Algunas de las combinaciones de sonidos que son útiles de practicar en inglés son /b/ y /v/, /v/ y /w/, y /l/ y /r/.

3. Resumen de tiras cómicas. Cuando su hijo/a haya terminado de leer una de sus historietas favoritas, pídale que le cuente en inglés de qué se trataba la historieta con palabras sencillas. Puede hacer lo mismo con los programas de dibujos animados que pasan por la televisión.

4. Todo lo que sabes. Establezca el hábito de leer el periódico y comentar con su hijo/a algunas de las noticias más importantes. Al final de la semana, mencione una de las noticias más importantes y pídale que le cuente en inglés todo lo que sepa acerca del tema.

NOTA: Si usted u otro miembro de la familia habla inglés, realice las actividades con su hijo/a en inglés. Si no sabe inglés, haga la parte que le corresponde en su propio idioma y pídale a su hijo que le responda en inglés.

Dear Parents,

A love of reading is the most valuable gift you can give your child because it is the foundation of success in school and in the workplace, as well as a source of personal pleasure. To help your child improve his or her reading skills, make sure your child knows that you value reading too. Let your child see you reading magazines, books, and newspapers with enjoyment. Keep age-appropriate reading material for your child and encourage him or her to read when you do. In addition, you can share the activities below.

1. Mighty Memory. This is a good, short game to play at the breakfast table or while riding in the car. Choose something on the table, such as a cereal box or the label from a jar of jam. (On the road, use billboards and signs.) Have your child read everything on the front of the box or on the label, studying it for one minute. Then ask him or her to repeat for you all the information he or she can remember. Take turns or invite others to play too.

2. Sharp Eyes. Magazine ads, newspaper ads, and menus work well for this game. Choose a word from somewhere on the page, tell your child what it is, and then give him or her thirty seconds to find that word.

3. TV Views. Have your child read descriptions of two or three TV programs that are on at the same time and then help you decide which program to watch, based on his or her descriptions and comments.

4. Guess. Help your child develop the skill of prediction by using the magazines and books you have at home. Show your child only the title of the magazine article or the title of the book and have him or her guess what the article or book will be about. Then, read a little together to find out if the prediction was correct. Ask your child what words or ideas helped him or her to predict an accurate answer.

NOTE: If you or other family members know English, do the activities in English with your child. If you do not, do them in your own language, and they will still help your child focus on strategies that will eventually transfer to better reading skills in English.

Estimados padres de familia:

El amor a la lectura es el regalo más valioso que usted puede darle a sus hijos, porque es la base del éxito escolar y laboral, así como una fuente de placer personal. Para ayudar a su hijo o hija a mejorar sus destrezas de lectura, demuéstrele que a usted también le gusta leer. Lea revistas, libros y periódicos con gusto frente a su hijo/a. Mantenga material de lectura apropiado para la edad de su hijo/a y anímelo a leer mientras usted lee. Además, pueden realizar juntos las siguientes actividades.

1. ¡Qué buena memoria! Este es un juego corto, muy apropiado para la hora del desayuno o cuando van en el auto. Elija algo que hay en la mesa, tal como una caja de cereal o la etiqueta de un frasco de mermelada. (Si van en el auto, use avisos publicitarios o señales.) Pida a su hijo/a que lea todo lo que hay en la parte frontal de la caja o en la etiqueta durante un minuto. Después, pídale que le repita toda la información  que recuerde. Túrnense para jugar o inviten a otros a jugar con ustedes.

2. Ojos de águila. Para este juego son muy adecuados avisos de revistas y periódicos o un menú. Elija una palabra de la página, dígale a su hijo/a cuál es la palabra y dele treinta segundos para encontrarla.

3. Programas de TV. Pida a su hijo/a que lea la descripción de dos o tres programas de televisión que se transmiten a la misma hora. Pídale que le ayude a decidir qué programa ver basándose en sus descripciones o comentarios.

4. Adivina. Use revistas y libros que tiene en su casa para ayudarle a su hijo/a a desarrollar la destreza de la predicción. Muéstrele tan sólo el título del artículo o del libro y pídale que adivine de qué se tratará. Después, lean juntos una parte para averiguar si la predicción fue correcta. Pregunte a su hijo/a qué palabras o ideas le ayudaron a acertar en su respuesta.

NOTA: Si usted u otro miembro de la familia habla inglés, realice las actividades en inglés junto con su hijo/a. Si no sabe inglés, hágalas en su propio idioma porque de cualquier forma le ayudarán a su hijo/a a desarrollar estrategias que le permitirán mejorar su habilidad para leer en inglés.

Dear Parents,

Reading is one of the most important skills in the world today because it is essential for success in the classroom and in the work world. As parents, you can provide your child with opportunities to read in English outside the classroom. Sharing a few reading activities at home is a wonderful way to show your child that reading is enjoyable as well as a source of knowledge. Encourage your child to read something in English every day, even if it is only a headline or two from the newspaper or a caption under a cartoon.

1. Mix and Match. Cut out several cartoons together with their captions from magazines and newspapers. Separate the captions from the cartoons and mix all the cartoons and captions in a pile on the table. Have your child match up each cartoon with its caption.

2. Memory Markers. Help your child form the good reading habit of asking the Wh- questions—who, what, when, where, and why—for any story or article. Have your child make a special bookmark for each book he or she reads with the title and this basic information on one side and his or her own drawing from a scene in the story or book on the other side. To preserve the bookmark, cover it with a transparent adhesive material. Encourage your child to collect as many bookmarks as possible during the year.

3. Scavenger Hunt. To help your child practice the important reading skill called scanning, choose an age-appropriate story or article and take ten details/facts from it. Make up ten questions, such as "Who did Jack visit after school?" or "What day was Sally's birthday?" or "What was the name of Charlie's dog?"—one question for each of the details or facts. Then have your child look quickly through the text to find only the information to answer each question. Have him or her tell you the page number where he or she found the answer.

NOTE: If you or other family members know English, do the activities in English with your child. If you do not, do them in your own language, and they will still help your child focus on strategies that will eventually transfer to better reading skills in English.

Estimados padres de familia:

La lectura es una de las destrezas más importantes en el mundo actual, puesto que es indispensable para el éxito escolar y laboral. Como padres, ustedes pueden brindarle a su hijo o hija oportunidades de leer en inglés fuera del salón de clase. El compartir algunas actividades de lectura en la casa es una magnífica forma de mostrarle a su hijo/a que la lectura es agradable además de ser fuente de conocimientos. Anime a su hijo/a a leer algo en inglés todos los días, aunque sólo sea uno o dos títulos del periódico o la leyenda de una tira cómica.

1. Revolver y unir. Recorte varias tiras cómicas de revistas o periódicos. Separe las leyendas de los dibujos y revuelva todos los dibujos y leyendas en un montón sobre la mesa. Pida a su hijo/a que una cada dibujo con su respectiva leyenda.

2. Recuerdos de lecturas. Ayude a su hijo/a a adquirir el buen hábito de hacerse las preguntas claves "quién, qué, cuándo, dónde y por qué" cada vez que lee un cuento o artículo. Pídale que haga un marcador especial por cada libro que lea, con el título y la información básica en un lado y un dibujo de una escena del cuento o libro en el otro lado. Para conservar el marcador de libros, cúbralo con un forro transparente tipo Contact™. Anime a su hijo/a a reunir todos los marcadores de libros que pueda durante el año.

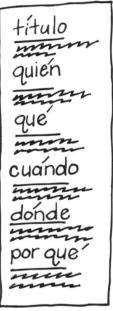

3. Búsqueda de datos. Para ayudar a su hijo/a a practicar la importante destreza de "sondear" al leer, elija un cuento o artículo apropiado para la edad del niño y saque diez detalles o datos del mismo. Formule una pregunta por cada detalle o dato hasta completar diez preguntas, como por ejemplo: "¿A quién visitó Jack después de la escuela?" o "¿En qué día cumple años Sally?" o "¿Cuál era el nombre del perro de Charlie?" Después, pida a su hijo/a que vea rápidamente el texto para hallar sólo la información que responda a cada pregunta. Pídale que le diga el número de la página donde encontró la respuesta.

NOTA: Si usted u otro miembro de la familia habla inglés, realice las actividades en inglés con su hijo/a. Si no sabe inglés, hágalas en su propio idioma porque de cualquier forma le ayudarán a su hijo/a a desarrollar estrategias que le permitirán mejorar su habilidad para leer en inglés.

Dear Parents,

As parents, you want your child to succeed in school and later in life. One important way you can help your child's chances of success is to encourage him or her to read as often as possible, both in his or her native language and in English. Set aside some time to read together and to talk about what you are reading. Let your child see the many different kinds of things that we read: newspapers, magazines, books, letters, product labels, notes, shopping lists, instruction manuals, dictionaries, and so on. Reading is a "real-life" skill.

1. Family Riddles. Using information and/or items from home, write out short riddles on index cards for your child to read and answer. Award one point for each right answer and a small prize such as a piece of gum for five points. For example, you may say, "I live in your sister's room. I am smaller than her teddy bear but taller than her jewelry box. I have my own car and many beautiful clothes. Who am I?" (the sister's favorite doll). In addition, pets, family stories, and relatives can be used as a basis for the riddles.

2. Reading Cards. This activity works well when you read aloud to your child. Have a stack of cards prepared with questions that will encourage the child to focus on the story. Tell him or her that every once in a while you will stop the story so that he or she can take the card on the top of the pile and answer it. (Make sure the cards are ordered correctly for the story.) The cards should have such questions as "If you were the main character, what would you do?" or "What do you think will happen next?" or "Why did the main character do that? Did that character make a good decision?", and so on.

3. Media Savvy. Listen to a news item on TV and then read about that same item in the newspaper. Have your child tell you the similarities and differences in the way the news item was discussed.

NOTE: If you or other family members know English, do the activities in English with your child. If you do not, do them in your own language, and they will still help your child focus on strategies that will eventually transfer to better reading skills in English.

Estimados padres de familia:

Como padres, deseamos que nuestros hijos triunfen en la escuela y en su vida futura. Una forma muy importante de fomentar el potencial de éxito de su hijo o hija es animarlo a que lea con la mayor frecuencia posible, tanto en su idioma natal como en inglés. Dediquen tiempo a leer juntos y a comentar lo que han leído. Muéstrele los muchos tipos de materiales que hay para leer: periódicos, revistas, libros, cartas, etiquetas de productos, notas, listas de compras, manuales de instrucciones, diccionarios, etc. La lectura es una destreza "cotidiana".

1. **Acertijos familiares.** Usando información u objetos del hogar, escriba acertijos cortos en tarjetas blancas para que su hijo/a los lea y adivine. Concédale un punto por cada respuesta correcta y un pequeño premio (como una goma de mascar) por cada cinco puntos. Por ejemplo, usted podría decir: "Vivo en la habitación de tu hermana. Soy más pequeña que su osito de peluche pero más alta que su cajita de joyas. Tengo mi propio auto y mucha ropa bonita. ¿Quién soy?" (la muñeca favorita de la hermana). Además puede usar datos de mascotas, anécdotas familiares y parientes como base para otros acertijos.

2. **Tarjetas de lectura.** Esta actividad es muy apropiada al leerle a su hijo/a en voz alta. Tenga a la mano un montón de tarjetas relacionadas con el cuento. Dígale que de vez en cuando usted suspenderá el cuento para que él o ella tome la primera tarjeta del montón y la responda. (Asegúrese de que las tarjetas estén en el orden correcto del cuento.) Las tarjetas deben contener preguntas tales como "Si tú fueras el personaje principal, ¿qué harías?" o "¿Qué crees que pasará después?" o "¿Por qué hizo eso el personaje principal? ¿Crees que fue una buena decisión?", y así sucesivamente.

3. **Noticias de aquí y de allá.** Escuchen una noticia por la televisión y lean acerca de ese mismo hecho en el periódico. Pida a su hijo/a que le diga las similitudes y diferencias en el modo en que la noticia fue tratada.

NOTA: Si usted u otro miembro de la familia habla inglés, realice las actividades en inglés con su hijo/a. Si no sabe inglés, hágalas en su propio idioma porque de cualquier forma le ayudarán a su hijo/a a desarrollar estrategias que le permitirán mejorar su habilidad para leer en inglés.

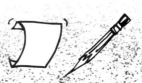

Dear Parents,

Reading brings pleasure as well as knowledge, yet many children dislike it because they lack confidence in their reading skills. You can help your child make progress in reading English through having books about his or her interests around the house and through sharing some entertaining activities at home. Spending some time each week reading or doing reading skills activities with your child will help him or her become a better reader of English and more likely to succeed in other academic subjects as well.

1. Movie Date. Involve your child in reading with a "real-life" purpose by assigning him or her some movie reviews or summaries to read. Let your child note the good and bad points of the movies and then make a recommendation for the family. Go to the movie he or she suggests if at all possible.

2. Zoo Research. Let your child know that you will visit the zoo on a specific date. Have him or her choose a favorite animal in the zoo to read about beforehand. Ask him or her to prepare a list of five, ten, or fifteen facts about that animal and to present the facts at the zoo while standing in front of the animal in question.

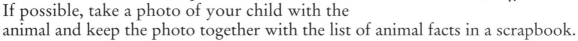

If possible, take a photo of your child with the animal and keep the photo together with the list of animal facts in a scrapbook.

3. Map Facts. To help your child read maps correctly, make a list of five to ten true/false questions, the answers to which can be found on a map (a city map, state map, map of the country, map of the world, etc.). Have him or her answer the questions first, predicting the answers, and then have your child check his or her predictions by finding the information on the map. For example, for a map of the United States, you may say, "Texas is between New Mexico and Louisiana" (true), "Nebraska is by the Great Lakes" (false), "The capital of Michigan is Lansing" (true), and so on.

NOTE: If you or other family members know English, do the activities in English with your child. If you do not, do them in your own language, and they will still help your child focus on strategies that will eventually transfer to better reading skills in English.

Estimados padres de familia:

La lectura es fuente de placer y conocimientos. Sin embargo, a muchos niños no les gusta porque no tienen confianza en sus destrezas de lectura. Para ayudarle a su hijo o hija a mejorar su lectura en inglés, tenga en la casa libros sobre sus temas de interés y comparta algunas actividades entretenidas en el hogar. El dedicar un rato cada semana a leer con su hijo/a o a hacer actividades que fomenten las destrezas de lectura, le ayudará a convertirse en un mejor lector en inglés y a su vez tendrá más probabilidades de triunfar en otras asignaturas académicas.

1. Comentarista de cine. Para motivar a su hijo/a a leer con un propósito "real", pídale que lea algunos comentarios o reseñas de películas de cine. Sugiérale que se base en las partes positivas y negativas de las películas para hacerle una recomendación a la familia. Si es posible, vayan a ver la película recomendada por su hijo/a.

2. Hacia el zoológico. Cuéntele a su hijo/a que irán al zoológico en una fecha determinada. Pídale que lea con anticipación acerca del animal que más le gusta del zoológico y que prepare una lista de cinco, diez o quince datos acerca de ese animal para presentarlos en el zoológico mientras lo ven. Si es posible, tome una foto de su hijo/a con el animal y guarde en un álbum la foto y la lista de datos.

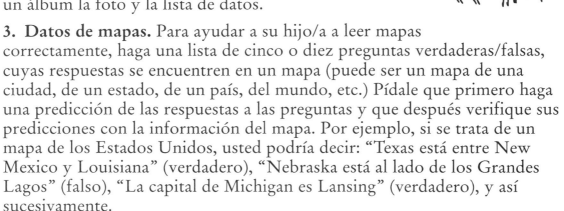

3. Datos de mapas. Para ayudar a su hijo/a a leer mapas correctamente, haga una lista de cinco o diez preguntas verdaderas/falsas, cuyas respuestas se encuentren en un mapa (puede ser un mapa de una ciudad, de un estado, de un país, del mundo, etc.) Pídale que primero haga una predicción de las respuestas a las preguntas y que después verifique sus predicciones con la información del mapa. Por ejemplo, si se trata de un mapa de los Estados Unidos, usted podría decir: "Texas está entre New Mexico y Louisiana" (verdadero), "Nebraska está al lado de los Grandes Lagos" (falso), "La capital de Michigan es Lansing" (verdadero), y así sucesivamente.

NOTA: Si usted u otro miembro de la familia habla inglés, realice las actividades en inglés con su hijo/a. Si no sabe inglés, hágalas en su propio idioma porque de cualquier forma le ayudarán a su hijo/a a desarrollar estrategias que le permitirán mejorar su habilidad para leer en inglés.

Dear Parents,

Writing is one of the most important skills your child will need in order to succeed in school and in later life. You can help your child by making writing a visible activity at home. Let your child see you writing letters, making lists, writing checks, filling out forms, sending e-mail, and writing in a diary or journal.

Writing as a language-learning skill involves several different aspects. For some English students, a new alphabet must be learned. Other students must learn to write from left to right on the page. Other students may know the English alphabet but must learn a new order of words in their sentences. In addition to these basic aspects, writing also involves such ideas as who we are writing for and why we are writing.

1. Alphabet Practice. For a child just learning the English alphabet and numbers, provide one or more of the following for practice in making the new shapes. Have a box of sand or rice where letters can be traced. Provide soft clay both to shape into letters and to mark with a stylus. Have poster paper and colorful fingerpaints ready. Provide stencil cutouts of letters and numbers that can be used to decorate a special box or corner of a room. Help your child shape cookie dough into letters and numbers, and then bake to eat.

2. Mystery Word. Trace a simple word in English with your finger on your child's back. Let him or her guess what word you wrote. Then allow him or her to do the same on your back. Repeat using different words.

3. Family Photos. Share a favorite photograph album with your child. Talk about the items and people in the pictures. Then have your child write a one- or two-sentence description or caption to paste under each photo.

NOTE: If you or other family members know English, do the activities in English with your child. If you do not, do them in your own language, and they will still help your child focus on strategies that will eventually transfer to better writing development in English.

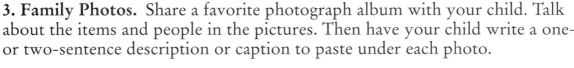

Estimados padres de familia:

La escritura es una de las destrezas más importantes que su hijo o hija necesitará para triunfar en la escuela y en su vida futura. Usted puede ayudarle destacando la acción de escribir en la casa. Escriba cartas, haga listas, escriba cheques, complete formularios, envíe mensajes por la computadora y escriba en un diario en presencia de su hijo/a.

La escritura como parte de la destreza para aprender un idioma comprende diversos aspectos. Algunos estudiantes de inglés deben aprender un nuevo alfabeto. Otros deben aprender a escribir de izquierda a derecha en la página. Otros estudiantes pueden saber el alfabeto inglés, pero deben aprender a ordenar las palabras en una oración de un nuevo modo. Además de estos aspectos básicos, la escritura también comprende ideas tales como a quién le estamos escribiendo y por qué estamos escribiendo.

1. ¡A practicar el alfabeto! Si su hijo/a apenas está aprendiendo el alfabeto y los números en inglés, tenga a la mano uno o más de los siguientes objetos para que pueda ensayar las nuevas figuras: Una caja con arena o arroz donde pueda trazar las letras; plastilina blanda ya sea para hacer las letras o para labrarlas con un punzón; cartulina y pintura dactilar de varios colores; figuras de letras y números que se puedan usar para decorar una caja o un rincón especial de una habitación. También podrían cortar juntos galletitas con forma de letras y números para hornearlas y saborearlas.

2. La palabra misteriosa. Trace con el dedo una palabra simple en inglés en la espalda de su hijo/a. Pídale que adivine qué palabra escribió usted. Después permítale que haga lo mismo en su espalda. Repitan la actividad con distintas palabras.

3. Fotos familiares. Vea un álbum favorito de fotos con su hijo/a. Hablen sobre los sitios y personas que aparecen en las fotos. Después pida a su hijo/a que escriba una descripción o leyenda de una o dos oraciones para pegar debajo de cada foto.

NOTA: Si usted u otro miembro de la familia habla inglés, realice las actividades en inglés con su hijo/a. Si no sabe inglés, hágalas en su propio idioma porque de cualquier forma le ayudarán a su hijo/a a desarrollar estrategias que le permitirán escribir mejor en inglés.

Dear Parents,

A large part of any student's success at school depends on developing effective reading and writing skills. As parents, you can provide your child with additional opportunities to improve his or her writing skills in English in the relaxed environment of the home. Spending some time each week on writing will help your child develop more self-confidence and ease of expression. The writing skills and strategies your child practices at home will serve him or her well both in school and in the workplace.

1. Ads. As preparation, have your child look at several advertisements for items popular with his or her age group, such as toys, clothing, sports equipment, music, and so on. Next have your child choose a favorite item he or she would like to buy, then design and write an ad for it. Display the ads your child does from time to time on a bulletin board or wall.

2. Fan Letters. Find out which singers, musical groups, film stars, sports figures, and TV personalities your child admires. Help him or her write a fan letter to a favorite person. Find out where you can send the letter and mail it. Many fan letters get replies, and sometimes even a picture; keep trying until your child gets a response. You may want to display a copy of the fan letter and any reply.

3. Story Words. Prepare slips of paper, each of which has one word. Write several verbs, some nouns, and some adjectives on the paper slips. Put them in an envelope and give it to your child. Have him or her write a story using all of the words from the envelope.

4. Postcards. Give your child a number of postcards with pictures of exotic places on them. Tell your child to imagine that he or she is there. Have him or her write a description of a typical day's activities for each place.

NOTE: If you or other family members know English, do the activities in English with your child. If you do not, do them in your own language, and they will still help your child focus on strategies that will eventually transfer to better writing development in English.

Estimados padres de familia:

Gran parte del éxito en la escuela depende del desarrollo efectivo de las destrezas de lectura y escritura. Como padres, ustedes pueden brindarle a su hijo o hija oportunidades adicionales para mejorar sus destrezas de escritura en inglés dentro del ambiente hogareño. El dedicar un rato cada semana a escribir le ayudará a su hijo/a adquirir más confianza en sí mismo/a y mayor facilidad de expresión. Las destrezas y estrategias de escritura que su hijo/a practique en casa, le servirán tanto en la escuela como en el mundo laboral.

1. Avisos. Como preparativo, pida a su hijo/a que mire varios avisos publicitarios de objetos populares entre chicos de su edad, tales como juguetes, ropa, equipos deportivos, música, etc. Después, pídale a su hijo/a que elija el objeto que más le gustaría comprar y que diseñe y escriba un aviso para promocionarlo. Exhiba de vez en cuando los avisos que su hijo/a haga en un tablero de anuncios.

2. Cartas de fanáticos. Averigüe cuáles son los cantantes, grupos musicales, estrellas de cine, figuras deportivas y personalidades de la televisión que su hijo/a admira más. Ayúdele a escribir una carta a uno de sus personajes favoritos. Averigüe a dónde puede enviarle la carta y póngala al correo. A veces las personalidades responden a estas cartas e incluso envían fotos a sus admiradores. Siga intentando hasta que su hijo/a obtenga una respuesta. Puede exhibir una copia de la carta y de la respuesta que reciba.

3. Cuentos. Prepare tiras de papel, cada una con una palabra. Incluya varios verbos, algunos sustantivos y algunos adjetivos en las tiras de papel. Póngalas en un sobre y entréguelas a su hijo/a. Pídale que escriba un cuento usando todas las palabras del sobre.

4. Tarjetas postales. Dé a su hijo/a algunas tarjetas postales con ilustraciones de lugares exóticos. Pídale que imagine que está en ese lugar y que escriba una descripción de las actividades que realiza en un día típico en cada lugar.

NOTA: Si usted u miembro de la familia habla inglés, realice las actividades en inglés con su hijo/a. Si no sabe inglés, hágalas en su propio idioma porque de cualquier forma le ayudarán a su hijo/a a desarrollar estrategias que le permitirán escribir mejor en inglés.

Dear Parents,

As parents, you want your child to have every opportunity for success. In school, success depends on good reading and writing skills. You can help your child develop his or her writing skills in English by sharing some fun activities at home. The effort you make now to encourage your child in writing will result in better preparation for later academic work and in a greater opportunity for success in later life. Encourage your child by showing him or her the importance of communicating well in "real life."

1. Picture Story. Cut out several magazine pictures and give them to your child. Have him or her use one or more as the setting for a story to write. Display the pictures and story on his or her bedroom wall.

2. Paragraph Structure. The basic English paragraph has a specific organization. Each paragraph has a main idea, which is stated in the first sentence. This sentence is followed by several other sentences that give details or more information about the main idea. Help your child identify main ideas and details by looking at written paragraphs together. Have him or her point to the sentence with the main idea and to the sentences with details.

3. Family Story. Tell your child a family story, such as how Grandfather and Grandmother met. Have your child draw a picture or two to illustrate the story, and then have him or her write the story to accompany the pictures.

4. Official Secretary. Help your child practice writing by dictating family notes, such as a shopping list for the grocery store or a list of chores to do on the weekend. Have him or her write notes to other family members about things they have to do (and a few words of thanks if they do them!).

NOTE: If you or other family members know English, do the activities in English with your child. If you do not, do them in your own language, and they will still help your child focus on strategies that will eventually transfer to better writing development in English.

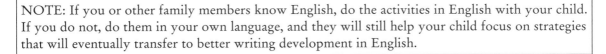

Estimados padres de familia:

Como padres queremos que nuestros hijos tengan todas las oportunidades de triunfar. El éxito escolar depende de buenas destrezas de lectura y escritura. Usted puede ayudar a su hijo o hija a desarrollar sus destrezas de escritura en inglés realizando juntos divertidas actividades en el hogar. El esfuerzo que usted haga ahora para estimular a su hijo/a a que escriba, lo preparará mejor para el trabajo académico y le dará una mayor oportunidad de tener éxito en el futuro. Anime a su hijo/a mostrándole la importancia de comunicarse bien en la "vida real".

1. **Cuentos ilustrados.** Recorte varias ilustraciones de revistas y déselas a su hijo/a. Pídale que use una o más como escenario para escribir un cuento. Exhiba las ilustraciones y el cuento en la pared de la habitación de su hijo/a.

2. **Estructura de un párrafo**. El párrafo básico en inglés tiene una organización específica. Cada párrafo tiene una idea principal, que se establece en la primera oración. Esta oración es seguida por varias oraciones que dan detalles o más información acerca de la idea principal. Ayude a su hijo/a a identificar las ideas principales y los detalles leyendo juntos varios párrafos. Pídale que señale la oración con la idea principal y las oraciones con los detalles.

3. **Relato familiar.** Cuéntele a su hijo/a un relato familiar, por ejemplo cómo se conocieron el abuelo y la abuela. Pídale que haga uno o dos dibujos para ilustrar el relato y que después escriba el relato.

4. **Secretario oficial.** Para estimular a su hijo/a a que escriba, díctele notas domésticas, como una lista de compras o una lista de quehaceres para hacer en el fin de semana. Pídale que escriba notas a otros miembros de la familia acerca de cosas que deben hacer (y unas palabras de agradecimiento por los oficios cumplidos.)

NOTA: Si usted u otro miembro de la familia habla inglés, realice las actividades en inglés con su hijo/a. Si no sabe inglés, hágalas en su propio idioma porque de cualquier forma le ayudarán a su hijo/a a desarrollar estrategias que le permitirán escribir mejor en inglés.

Dear Parents,

Helping your child develop an appreciation of writing is one of the most valuable things you can do to encourage academic success. Now your child is learning to write in English, a skill that takes time and practice. You can help your child improve his or her writing by sharing some fun activities at home. Setting aside a few minutes each week to practice writing will help your child develop the skills he or she needs to do well in school and in life.

1. Story Mixes. Have your child name his or her favorite characters from two different stories. Then have him or her write a new story that has both characters in it. For example, he or she may write a new story with both Cinderella and Superman. Encourage the use of imagination in writing.

2. Story Turns. Take turns writing a story with your child. Begin by writing the first sentence, have your child write the next sentence, then you write the next sentence, and so on. Help him or her be logical and follow a story line. This activity can be one short story or a longer story that both of you contribute to each week until it is finished.

3. Paragraph Strips. Help your child understand the organization of an English paragraph. Write a simple paragraph on several strips of paper, each strip containing a complete sentence. Mix up the strips, and then have your child arrange the strips in the correct order. Ask him or her what clues he or she identified to help in arranging the sentences.

4. Advice. Many magazines and newspapers have advice columns, where people talk about their problems and ask for advice. Choose a letter and have your child write a letter in response, giving his or her ideas about solving the problem. You can also do this with family problems.

NOTE: If you or other family members know English, do the activities in English with your child. If you do not, do them in your own language, and they will still help your child focus on strategies that will eventually transfer to better writing development in English.

Estimados padres de familia:

El ayudar a su hijo o hija a desarrollar el gusto por la escritura es una de las mejores cosas que puede hacer para estimular su éxito académico. Su hijo/a está aprendiendo a escribir en inglés, una destreza que necesita tiempo y práctica. Usted puede ayudar a su hijo/a a mejorar su escritura realizando divertidas actividades en el hogar. El dedicar unos cuantos minutos a la semana a practicar la escritura le ayudará a su hijo/a a desarrollar las destrezas que necesitará para que triunfe en la escuela y en la vida en general.

1. Mezcla de cuentos. Pida a su hijo/a que diga cuáles son sus personajes favoritos de dos cuentos diferentes. Después pídale que escriba un nuevo cuento en el que aparezcan ambos personajes. Por ejemplo, podría escribir un nuevo cuento con Cenicienta y Superman. Anímelo/a a usar la imaginación.

2. Por turnos. Túrnense con su hijo/a para escribir un cuento. Comience por escribir la primera oración, pida a su hijo/a que escriba la siguiente oración, después usted escribe la siguiente y así sucesivamente. Ayúdele a seguir un orden lógico y a ser coherente. Esta actividad puede dar como resultado un cuento corto o un cuento largo al que ambos contribuyen cada semana hasta terminarlo.

3. Tiras de párrafos. Ayude a su hijo/a a entender la organización de un párrafo en inglés. Elija un párrafo simple y córtelo en tiras, cada una con una oración completa. Mezcle las tiras y después pida a su hijo/a que las coloque en el orden correcto. Pregúntele qué claves le ayudaron a identificar el orden de las oraciones.

4. Consejos. Muchas revistas y periódicos tienen columnas de consejos, donde la gente habla acerca de sus problemas y pide ayuda. Elija una de estas cartas y pida a su hijo/a que escriba una carta de respuesta, dando sus ideas de cómo resolver el problema. Podrían hacer lo mismo con problemas familiares.

NOTA: Si usted u otro miembro de la familia habla inglés, realice las actividades en inglés con su hijo/a. Si no sabe inglés, hágalas en su propio idioma porque de cualquier forma le ayudarán a su hijo/a a desarrollar estrategias que le permitirán escribir mejor en inglés.

Dear Parents,

A strong vocabulary is an important part of successful speaking, reading, and writing, both in school and in the workplace. As your child studies English, he or she will learn many new words. This growth in vocabulary will help your child not only with English, but also with other subjects such as history and science. Through sharing activities at home, you can encourage your child to feel confident learning and using new words.

1. Post-ups. Use small pieces of paper or index cards for this activity. Choose a logical grouping of words, such as furniture or colors. Write one word on each paper, mix them up in a paper bag, and then have your child pull out the words and find the matching items. Have him or her tape the word to the actual item so that each real-life item is labeled. To make it more exciting, give your child a time limit or a small prize.

2. Odd Word Out. This is fun in the car or at the dinner table. Call out a group of four or five words, one of which does not logically belong. Have your child identify the odd word and tell why it doesn't belong. For example, you might say, "shoe, boot, slipper, pencil, sandal." Your child would identify *pencil* as the odd word because all the other words are types of footwear.

3. Middles. Tell your child that you are thinking of a word but that you can only provide the first and last letter of the word. (This can be done orally or on paper.) Have your child guess the missing letters by asking you questions about the word. For example, you might be thinking of the word *mouse*. Your child would only know the letters *m* and *e.* He or she might ask if the word is an action (no), an animal (yes), and so on. You can provide clues, such as "Cats like to chase this animal."

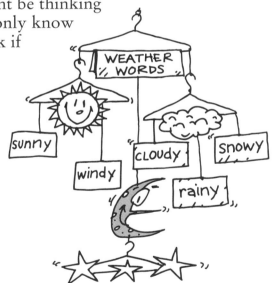

4. Word Mobiles. With a hanger or two and some thread, your child can construct mobiles from which hang groups of related words. For example, one hanger might have only words related to sports, another might have words related to music and musical instruments, and so on.

NOTE: If you or other family members speak English, do the activities in English with your child. If you do not, do them in your own language, and they will still help your child focus on strategies that will eventually transfer to better vocabulary development in English.

Estimados padres de familia:

Un vocabulario sólido es parte importante del éxito al hablar, leer y escribir, tanto en la escuela como en el mundo laboral. A medida que su hijo o hija estudia inglés, aprenderá muchas palabras nuevas. Este aumento en su vocabulario le ayudará no sólo con el inglés en sí, sino también con otras asignaturas como historia y ciencias. Usted puede estimular a su hijo/a a que aprenda y use nuevas palabras con confianza realizando juntos algunas actividades.

1. Letreros. Use trozos pequeños de papel, tarjetas en blanco o notas adhesivas para esta actividad. Elija un grupo lógico de palabras, tales como muebles o colores. Escriba una palabra en cada papel, revuélvalos en una bolsa de papel y después pida a su hijo/a que saque las palabras y que encuentre los objetos equivalentes. Pídale que pegue la palabra al objeto correspondiente de tal forma que cada cosa tenga su letrero. Para entusiasmar a su hijo/a, fije un límite de tiempo o concédale un pequeño premio.

2. Palabra ajena. Éste es un juego divertido para el auto o la mesa de comer. Mencione un grupo de cuatro o cinco palabras, una de la cuales no pertenece al grupo por lógica. Pida a su hijo/a que identifique la palabra que no pertenece al grupo y que explique por qué. Por ejemplo, usted podría decir "zapato, bota, pantufla, lápiz, sandalia". Su hijo/a diría que el lápiz es la palabra que no pertenece al grupo porque todas las demás son nombres de calzado.

3. Adivina la palabra. Diga a su hijo/a que usted está pensando en una palabra pero que sólo le dará la primera y la última letra de la palabra. (Esto se puede hacer oralmente o por escrito.) Pida a su hijo/a que adivine las letras que faltan haciéndole a usted preguntas acerca de esa palabra. Por ejemplo, usted podría pensar en la palabra *ratón*. Su hijo/a tan sólo conocerá las letras *r* y *n*. Podría preguntar si la palabra es una acción (no), un animal (sí), y así sucesivamente. Usted puede darle pistas como "A los gatos les gusta perseguir a este animal".

4. Móvil de palabras. Con un gancho de colgar ropa y cordel, su hijo/a puede hacer móviles para colgar grupos de palabras relacionadas. Por ejemplo, un gancho podría tener tan sólo palabras relacionadas con deportes, otro podría tener palabras relacionadas con música e instrumentos musicales, y así sucesivamente.

NOTA: Si usted u otro miembro de la familia habla inglés, realice las actividades en inglés con su hijo/a. Si no sabe inglés, hágalas en su propio idioma porque de cualquier forma le ayudarán a su hijo/a a desarrollar estrategias que le permitirán enriquecer su vocabulario en inglés.

Dear Parents,

Encouraging your child to build a larger vocabulary in English is one important way you can help him or her become a better speaker, reader, and writer. A good vocabulary is necessary not only for success in school but also for success in the workplace later on. As parents, you can provide your child with additional opportunities to learn and use new vocabulary words in English by sharing the fun activities mentioned below.

1. Scrambled Words. Collect a number of pictures of individual items, such as a chair, a table, a lamp, and so on. For each picture, have a slip of paper. Write a scrambled version of each word on the slips and have your child unscramble each word and match it to the correct picture. For example, *chair* could be scrambled as *raich*, *table* as *blate*, and so on.

2. Lists. Choose a category such as "vegetables," "furniture," or "sports equipment." Have your child write down all the words related to that category that he or she can think of within a one-minute time limit. For younger children, the time limit can be longer. For example, for the category "tools," your child could list *hammer*, *saw*, *wrench*, *pliers*, and *drill*.

3. Guess the Word. Choose a category such as "musical instruments" or "fruit." Have your child guess the word in that category that you are thinking of by giving simple clues, such as "This fruit is round and red." (apple) Take turns guessing and giving clues.

4. Verb Flowers. English has many two-word verbs that consist of a verb and a preposition. Each combination has a different meaning. Help your child associate two-word verbs with their meanings. Draw (or have your child draw) a big daisy. In the center, write in the verb. On each petal, write a preposition that combines with the verb. Have your child write a definition on each petal. For example, in the center you may write *get*. On the petals would be *up*, *in*, *off*, *out*, *down*, *through*, and *on*.

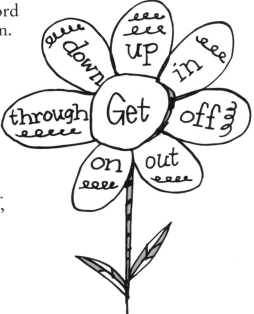

NOTE: If you or other family members speak English, do the activities in English with your child. If you do not, do them in your own language, and they will still help your child focus on strategies that will eventually transfer to better vocabulary development in English.

Estimados padres de familia:

El estimular a su hijo o hija a enriquecer su vocabulario en inglés es muy importante para ayudarle a ser un mejor orador, lector y escritor. Un buen vocabulario es necesario no sólo para el éxito escolar sino también para el éxito laboral. Como padres, ustedes pueden brindarle a su hijo/a oportunidades adicionales de aprender y de usar nuevas palabras en inglés realizando juntos las divertidas actividades que se sugieren a continuación.

1. Palabras revueltas. Reúna un grupo de ilustraciones de objetos individuales, tales como un silla, una mesa, una lámpara y cosas por el estilo. Por cada ilustración, tenga una tira de papel. En cada tira escriba una palabra con las letras revueltas e invite a su hijo/a a ordenar cada palabra y unirla con la ilustración correcta. Por ejemplo, la palabra *silla* se puede revolver como *llasi, mesa como sema* y así sucesivamente.

2. Listas. Elija una categoría tal como "vegetales", "muebles", o "equipo deportivo". Pida a su hijo/a que escriba todas las palabras que se le ocurran relacionadas con esa categoría durante un minuto. El límite de tiempo puede ser mayor cuando se trata de niños más pequeños. Por ejemplo, para la categoría "herramientas", su hijo/a podría anotar *martillo, serrucho, llave inglesa, alicates* y *taladro.*

3. Adivina la palabra. Elija una categoría tal como "instrumentos musicales" o "frutas". Pida a su hijo/a que adivine la palabra de esa categoría en la que usted está pensando, dándole pistas sencillas, tales como "Esta fruta es redonda y roja". (manzana) Túrnense para adivinar y dar pistas.

4. Flor de verbos. El inglés tiene muchos verbos de dos palabras que consisten de un verbo y una preposición. Cada combinación tiene un significado diferente. Ayude a su hijo/a a asociar verbos de dos palabras con su significado correspondiente. Dibuje (o pídale a su hijo/a que dibuje) una margarita grande. En el centro, escriba el verbo. En cada pétalo, escriba una preposición que combine con ese verbo. Pida a su hijo/a que escriba una definición en cada pétalo. Por ejemplo, en el centro usted podría escribir *get.* En los pétalos podría escribir *up, in, off, out, down, through* y *on.*

NOTA: Si usted u otro miembro de la familia habla inglés, realice las actividades en inglés con su hijo/a. Si no sabe inglés, hágalas en su propio idioma porque de cualquier forma le ayudarán a su hijo/a a desarrollar estrategias que le permitirán enriquecer su vocabulario en inglés.

Dear Parents,

A good vocabulary is one of the most important elements in speaking, reading, and writing in English. As parents, you can help your child develop a larger vocabulary in English by devoting some time each week to vocabulary-building skills at home. Sharing the challenging and fun activities below will increase your child's confidence in learning and using new words.

1. Word Hunt. Prepare a number of paper slips or index cards, each of which has a clue about a word. (All the words should be of things in the house.) Have your child go around the house and figure out which word you are referring to within a certain time limit. For example, one paper may read, "I'm in the kitchen. I begin with an *r* and I end with an *r*." (refrigerator) Another may read, "I'm in the living room. I begin with a *t* and I end with an *n*." (television)

2. Puzzle Pieces. Take several pieces of paper and cut out puzzle shapes (be sure the pieces can fit back together). On one piece, write a vocabulary word your child needs to know. On a connecting piece, write a simple definition. Do the same for all the remaining pieces. Mix up all the puzzle pieces and have your child put the puzzle back together by matching the words with their definitions. Save the puzzles and review them occasionally.

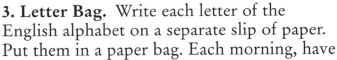

3. Letter Bag. Write each letter of the English alphabet on a separate slip of paper. Put them in a paper bag. Each morning, have your child pull out one of the letters and have him learn a new word beginning with that letter. You or your child can choose the word, or he or she can use a vocabulary word from his or her school lessons. Have your child define and use the new word for you at the end of the day.

4. Opposites. This is fun to do in the car or at the table. Say a word in English and have your child give you its opposite. For example, you may say, "tall," "hot," or "new." Your child would respond with "short," "cold," or "old."

NOTE: If you or other family members speak English, do the activities in English with your child. If you do not, do them in your own language, and they will still help your child focus on strategies that will eventually transfer to better vocabulary development in English.

Estimados padres de familia:

Un buen vocabulario es uno de los elementos más importantes para hablar, leer y escribir en inglés. Como padres, ustedes pueden ayudar a su hijo o hija a adquirir un vocabulario más amplio en inglés dedicando un rato de cada semana a promover ciertas destrezas. El realizar juntos las divertidas e interesantes actividades que se mencionan a continuación le permitirá a su hijo/a aprender y usar nuevas palabras con mayor seguridad.

1. Cacería de palabras. Prepare un grupo de tiras de papel o tarjetas de cartulina, cada una con una pista acerca de una palabra. (Todas las palabras deben ser de objetos que hay en la casa.) Pida a su hijo/a que vaya alrededor de la casa tratando de descubrir, dentro de cierto límite de tiempo, a que palabra se refiere usted. Por ejemplo, un papel podría decir: "Estoy en la cocina. Comienzo con una *r* y termino con una *r*. (refrigerador) Otro podría decir: "Estoy en la sala. Comienzo con una *t* y termino con una *r*. (televisor)

2. Piezas de rompecabezas. Recorte una hoja de papel en varias piezas de rompecabezas (asegúrese de que las piezas encajen al armarse.) En una pieza, escriba una palabra que su hijo/a necesite aprender. En otra pieza que conecte con la anterior, escriba una definición simple. Haga lo mismo con el resto de las piezas. Revuelva las piezas y pida a su hijo/a que arme el rompecabezas uniendo las palabra con su respectiva definición. Guarde los rompecabezas y véanlos de vez en cuando.

3. Bolsa de letras. Escriba cada letra del alfabeto inglés en una tira de papel aparte. Póngalas en una bolsa de papel. Cada mañana, pida a su hijo/a que saque una de las letras y que aprenda una nueva palabra que comience con esa letra. Usted o su hijo/a pueden elegir la palabra o usar el vocabulario que debe aprenderse para la escuela. Pida a su hijo/a que defina y use la nueva palabra al final del día.

4. Opuestos. Esta actividad es divertida en el auto o en la mesa. Diga una palabra en inglés y pida a su hijo/a que le dé su opuesto. Por ejemplo, usted podría decir "alto", "caliente", o "nuevo". Su hijo/a respondería "bajo", "frío" o "viejo".

NOTA: Si usted u otro miembro de la familia habla inglés, realice las actividades en inglés con su hijo/a. Si no sabe inglés, hágalas en su propio idioma porque de cualquier forma le ayudarán a su hijo/a a desarrollar estrategias que le permitirán enriquecer su vocabulario en inglés.

Dear Parents,

Successful speakers, readers, and writers all take advantage of every opportunity to learn and use new vocabulary words. As parents, you want your child to succeed in school, and you can help him or her build a larger vocabulary in English at home. Spend some time each week talking about words and their meanings; play word games and share the activities below.

1. Synonym Bingo. Prepare Bingo cards like the traditional ones, but with words instead of numbers in the spaces. For each word on the cards, have a synonym on a list. Have your child listen carefully as you call out a word from the list. He or she should then find the similar word on his or her Bingo card and mark it with an *X*. For example, you may call out "worried." Your child will look, find the word *upset* on his or her card, and mark it.

2. Rhyme Riddles. Prepare a list of words that rhyme. Use a word in a sentence as in "You cook food in me. I'm a pot." Give clues to another word on the list as in "I'm the opposite of cold." Your child would continue by finishing the idea with a rhyming word, saying, "I'm hot." Continue giving clues and guessing until you have used all the rhyming words on your list.

3. Word Families. Say a word or write it on a piece of paper. Have your child think of as many words in the same related family as possible. For example, if you say, "photograph," your child would say, "photo, photographer, photographic, photographically," and so on. Some words for this game include *use*, *critic*, *repeat*, and *benefit*.

4. Word Posters. Use pictures to have your child make a word poster. For example, if you give him or her a picture of a natural disaster such as a flood, he or she can paste the picture at the top of a large piece of paper and then fill the remaining space with words related to natural disasters, for example, *flood*, *tornado*, *fire*, *snowstorm*, *help*, *first aid*, *Red Cross*, *emergency*, and so on.

NOTE: If you or other family members know English, do the activities in English with your child. If you do not, do them in your own language, and they will still help your child focus on concepts that will eventually build a better awareness of grammar.

Estimados padres de familia:

Los buenos oradores, lectores y escritores aprovechan cualquier oportunidad de aprender y usar el vocabulario que han adquirido. Como padres, ustedes desean que su hijo o hija triunfe en la escuela. Para ayudarle en la casa a adquirir un vocabulario más amplio en inglés, dediquen un rato a la semana a hablar acerca de palabras y su significado; realicen juegos de palabras y compartan las siguientes actividades.

1. Bingo de sinónimos. Prepare cartones de Bingo como los tradicionales, pero con palabras en lugar de números. Por cada una de las palabras de los cartones, tenga un sinónimo en una lista. Pida a su hijo/a que escuche atentamente mientras usted menciona una palabra de la lista. Su hijo/a entonces debe buscar la palabra similar en su cartón de Bingo y marcarla con una X. Por ejemplo, usted podría decir "intranquilo". Su hijo/a ubicará la palabra *preocupado* en su cartón y la marcará.

2. Adivinanzas con rima. Prepare una lista de palabras que rimen. Haga una oración con una de esas palabras como "Con sal y cebolla, en mí se cocina la sopa. Soy la olla" Dé pistas para otra palabra de la lista como "Estoy frío como un helado". Su hijo/a terminará la idea con una palabra que rime diciendo "Estoy congelado". Siga dando pistas y adivinando hasta que haya usado todas las palabras que riman en su lista.

3. Familias de palabras. Diga una palabra o escríbala en una hoja de papel. Pida a su hijo/a que piense en todas las palabras que se lo ocurran de la misma familia. Por ejemplo, si usted dice "foto", su hijo/a diría "fotografía, fotógrafo, fotográfico, fotográficamente", y así sucesivamente. Algunas palabras que se pueden usar en este juego son *raro, repetir, moda* y *carne*.

4. Cartel de palabras. Suministre a su hijo/a ilustraciones para hacer un cartel de palabras. Por ejemplo, si usted le da una ilustración de un desastre natural tal como una inundación, su hijo/a puede pegar la ilustración en la parte superior de una hoja grande de papel y llenar el resto del espacio con palabras relacionadas con desastres naturales, como por ejemplo: *inundación, tornado, incendio, tormenta de nieve, ayuda, primeros auxilios, Cruz Roja, emergencia* y así sucesivamente.

NOTA: Si usted u otro miembro de la familia habla inglés, realice las actividades en inglés con su hijo/a. Si no sabe inglés, hágalas en su propio idioma porque de cualquier forma le ayudarán a su hijo/a a concentrarse en conceptos que le permitirán enriquecer su vocabulario en inglés.

Dear Parents,

All languages, no matter how simple or complex, have grammar rules. Whether easy or difficult to understand, these rules help us both form and comprehend communication. Without grammar, we would not be able to understand the meaning of our words, phrases, and sentences. A good understanding of grammar is essential for communication.

You can help your child become a more confident language-learner by reviewing and practicing the grammar rules and concepts being studied. As speakers of your native language, you can use what you know about its grammar rules to help your child see what is similar and what is different regarding the structure of English.

1. Grammar Words. This activity will help your child understand what each word does in an English sentence. First, familiarize yourself with the grammatical terms on pages 90–91, and then have your child give examples of them from sentences in a favorite story, magazine, or newspaper. For example, in the sentence "Bobby is watching TV", *Bobby* is both a noun and the subject of the sentence, *is watching* is the verb, and *TV* is both a noun and the object.

2. Scrambled Sentences. Write a few simple sentences in English or copy a few from your child's textbook. Cut up each sentence into separate words and then have your child arrange the words in their original order.

3. You Bet! To practice subject-verb agreement, say or write out some simple sentences, some of them correct, such as "You sing well", and some of them incorrect, such as "He sing well." Have your child bet (a bean, or a paper clip, etc.) on which ones are correct or incorrect. Have him or her tell you what the mistakes are in the incorrect examples, and then correct them.

NOTE: If you or other family members know English, do the activities in English with your child. If you do not, do them in your own language, and they will still help your child focus on concepts that will eventually build a better awareness of grammar.

Estimados padres de familia:

Todos los idiomas, por sencillos o complejos que sean, tienen reglas gramaticales. Estas reglas, sean fáciles o difíciles de entender, nos ayudan a comunicarnos y a comprender lo que nos comunican. Sin la gramática, no podríamos entender el significado de nuestras palabras, frases y oraciones. Una buena comprensión de la gramática es esencial para la comunicación.

Usted puede ayudar a su hijo o hija a adquirir más confianza en el aprendizaje del idioma revisando y practicando las reglas gramaticales y los conceptos que está estudiando. Pueden usar las reglas gramaticales de su idioma natal para ayudar a su hijo/a a ver qué similitudes y qué diferencias hay con respecto a la estructura en inglés.

1. Cuestión de gramática. Esta actividad ayudará a su hijo/a a entender la función de cada palabra en una oración en inglés. Primero, familiarícese con los términos gramaticales de las páginas 90-91, y después pídale a su hijo/a que dé ejemplos de esos términos sacados de oraciones de un cuento favorito, revista o periódico. Por ejemplo, en la oración "Bobby *está viendo* televisión", *Bobby* es tanto el sustantivo como el sujeto de la oración, *está viendo* es el verbo y *televisión* es tanto un sustantivo como el objeto.

2. Oraciones mezcladas. Escriba unas cuantas oraciones sencillas en inglés o copie algunas del libro de texto de su hijo/a. Corte cada oración en palabras separadas y después pida a su hijo/a que coloque las palabras en su orden original.

3. ¡Te apuesto! Para practicar la correspondencia entre sujeto y verbo, diga o escriba unas oraciones sencillas, algunas correctas como "Tú cantas bien", y otras incorrectas como "Él cantas bien". Pida a su hijo/a que haga una apuesta (un frijol, un sujetapapeles, etc.) de cuáles son correctas o incorrectas. Pídale que le diga qué error hay en los ejemplos incorrectos y que los corrija.

NOTA: Si usted u otro miembro de la familia habla inglés, realice las actividades en inglés con su hijo/a. Si no sabe inglés, hágalas en su propio idioma porque de cualquier forma le ayudarán a su hijo/a a concentrarse en conceptos que le permitirán tener un mejor dominio gramatical.

Dear Parents,

Understanding grammar is an extremely important part of learning a new language. Your child is learning English, and many of the grammar rules are probably different from the grammar rules in your native language. As parents, you can help your child master English grammar rules at home. Spending some time each week sharing a few grammar activities will help your child understand more of what he or she hears, reads, and writes.

1. Sense Verbs. To help your child become aware that verbs of the senses (look, sound, taste, smell, feel) are followed by adjectives, prepare a pile of pictures of items that can be used with sense verbs. Then have your child think of a list of appropriate adjectives such as *happy, sad, loud, terrible, sweet, salty, sour, rotten, delicious, soft, good, smooth,* and so on. Have your child form sentences using the pictures, such as "The lemon tastes sour./The kitten feels soft./The band sounds loud./The little girl looks happy" and so on.

2. Verb Spin. To practice several different verb tenses at a time, take a large sheet of paper and draw a big circle in the middle. Divide the circle into sections, one for each verb tense. Write the name of a verb tense (or an example of each verb tense) in each section. Place a small bottle on its side in the center of the circle to use as a spinner. Have your child spin the bottle and make a sentence using the verb tense in the section where the neck of the bottle points. For example, if the bottle points to "Past Tense," your child could say, "Yesterday, I played basketball with my friends."

3. Where Is It? Have your child practice prepositions of place by answering questions that require use of prepositions such as *in, on, near, under, above, next to, between,* and so on. For example, if you say, "Where is the white lamp?", your child would say, "By the couch."

NOTE: If you or other family members know English, do the activities in English with your child. If you do not, do them in your own language, and they will still help your child focus on concepts that will eventually build a better awareness of grammar.

Estimados padres de familia:

El entender la gramática es parte muy importante en el aprendizaje de un nuevo idioma. Su hijo o hija está aprendiendo inglés, y muchas de las reglas gramaticales probablemente son diferentes de las reglas de su idioma natal. Como padres, ustedes pueden ayudarle a su hijo/a en la casa a dominar las reglas gramaticales en inglés. El dedicar un tiempo cada semana a realizar juntos unas cuantas actividades de gramática, le ayudará a su hijo/a a entender mejor lo que escucha, lee y escribe.

1. Verbos sensoriales. Para ayudar a su hijo o hija a comprender que los verbos relacionados con los sentidos (vista, oído, gusto, olfato, tacto) están seguidos por adjetivos, prepare un montón de ilustraciones de objetos que se pueden usar con verbos sensoriales. Después pida a su hijo/a que piense en una lista de adjetivos apropiados tales como *feliz, triste, duro, terrible, dulce, salado, ácido, podrido, delicioso, suave, bueno, terso*, etc. Pida a su hijo/a que haga oraciones usando las ilustraciones, tales como "El limón sabe ácido"/La piel del gatito se siente suave/La orquesta suena duro/La niña se ve feliz" y así sucesivamente.

2. Ruleta de verbos. Para practicar diferentes tiempos verbales, tome una hoja grande de papel y dibuje un círculo grande en la mitad. Divida el círculo en secciones, una por cada tiempo verbal. Escriba el nombre de un tiempo verbal (o un ejemplo de cada tiempo verbal) en cada sección. Coloque una pequeña botella sobre un costado en el centro del círculo para usar como ruleta. Pida a su hijo/a que haga girar la botella y que diga una oración usando el tiempo verbal de la sección a la que el pico de la botella apunta. Por ejemplo, si la botella apunta al "Tiempo pasado", su hijo/a podría decir: "Ayer jugué al baloncesto con mis amigos".

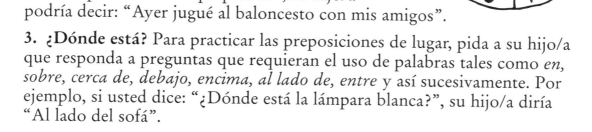

3. ¿Dónde está? Para practicar las preposiciones de lugar, pida a su hijo/a que responda a preguntas que requieran el uso de palabras tales como *en, sobre, cerca de, debajo, encima, al lado de, entre* y así sucesivamente. Por ejemplo, si usted dice: "¿Dónde está la lámpara blanca?", su hijo/a diría "Al lado del sofá".

NOTA: Si usted u otro miembro de la familia habla inglés, realice las actividades en inglés con su hijo/a. Si no sabe inglés, hágalas en su propio idioma porque de cualquier forma le ayudarán a su hijo/a a concentrarse en conceptos que le permitirán tener un mejor dominio gramatical.

Dear Parents:

Learning a new language requires the study of grammar rules in addition to speaking, reading, and writing. The more grammar your child can practice and use, the better he or she will understand spoken and written English. You can help your child review and consolidate the grammar he or she is studying at school in your home. Try sharing the activities below with your child.

1. Pronoun Partners. Help your child understand pronoun references using sentences from a favorite story or magazine. Find sentences that have subject pronouns in them (I, you, he, she, it, we, they) and have your child find the nouns they refer to. (These nouns may be in the same sentence or in previous sentences.) An example might be the following: "Batman and Robin heard the alarm. They jumped up and ran to the Batmobile." Your child would identify *Batman* and *Robin* as the nouns the word *they* refers to.

2. Card Game. Help your child practice making questions with *do* and giving short answers with "Yes, I do" and "No, I don't." Use two sets of playing cards or two sets of the same pictures or postcards. Mix them up and put them in a pile on the table. Give your child five cards (or pictures) and take five for yourself. Then ask your child, "Do you have a three of hearts?" (or a picture of a cat, and so on). If your child says, "No, I don't," take another card from the pile. If he or she says, "Yes, I do," you collect the card. The person with the higher number of identical cards (or pictures) wins the game.

3. A/An. Prepare a group of small objects or a pile of pictures. (Make sure that some begin with consonant sounds and some begin with vowel sounds; *a* is used before consonant sounds and *an* is used before vowel sounds.) Show your child the item and have him or her use the correct article before the word. For example, your child could say, "a pen" or "an apple."

NOTE: If you or other family members know English, do the activities in English with your child. If you do not, do them in your own language, and they will still help your child focus on concepts that will eventually build a better awareness of grammar.

Estimados padres de familia:

El aprendizaje de un nuevo idioma requiere el estudio de sus reglas gramaticales además de aprender a hablarlo, leerlo y escribirlo. Cuanta más gramática pueda practicar y usar su hijo/a, podrá entender mejor el inglés hablado y escrito. Ustedes pueden ayudarle a repasar y afianzar en la casa la gramática que está aprendiendo en la escuela. Trate de realizar las siguientes actividades con su hijo/a.

1. **Patrones de pronombres.** Ayude a su hijo/a entender la relación de los pronombres usando oraciones de un cuento o historieta favorita. Busque oraciones que tengan pronombres personales (yo, tú, él, ella, eso, nosotros, ellos) y pida a su hijo/a que busque los sustantivos a los que se refieren (Estos sustantivos podrían estar en la misma oración o en oraciones anteriores.) Un ejemplo podría ser: "Batman y Robin oyeron la alarma. Al oírla, ellos salieron corriendo al Batimóvil". Su hijo/a identificaría *Batman* y *Robin* como los sustantivos a los que la palabra *ellos* se refiere.

2. **Juego de cartas.** Ayude a su hijo/a a practicar preguntas con *tienes* (Do you Have…?) y a dar respuestas cortas con (Yes, I do) y (No, I don't.) Use dos juegos de naipes o dos juegos de ilustraciones o tarjetas postales iguales. Revuélvalas y póngalas en un montón sobre la mesa. Dé a su hijo/a cinco cartas (o ilustraciones) y tome cinco para usted. Después pregunte a su hijo/a: "¿Tienes un tres de corazones?" (o un dibujo de un gato, y así sucesivamente). Si su hijo/a dice, (No, I don't), usted toma otra carta del montón. Si dice (Yes, I do), usted toma la carta. La persona que tenga el mayor número de cartas (o ilustraciones) idénticas gana el juego.

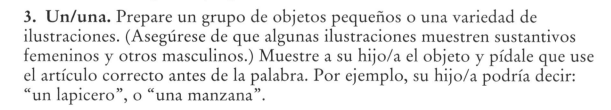

3. **Un/una.** Prepare un grupo de objetos pequeños o una variedad de ilustraciones. (Asegúrese de que algunas ilustraciones muestren sustantivos femeninos y otros masculinos.) Muestre a su hijo/a el objeto y pídale que use el artículo correcto antes de la palabra. Por ejemplo, su hijo/a podría decir: "un lapicero", o "una manzana".

NOTA: Si usted u otro miembro de la familia habla inglés, realice las actividades en inglés con su hijo/a. Si no sabe inglés, hágalas en su propio idioma porque de cualquier forma le ayudarán a su hijo/a a concentrarse en conceptos que le permitirán tener un mejor dominio gramatical.

Dear Parents,

We learn a new language to communicate. To communicate clearly, it is important to learn and use the grammar rules of a language correctly. You can provide your child with opportunities to practice English at home by spending some time each week doing grammar activities such as the ones suggested below. Extra grammar practice will help your child become a better English speaker, reader, and writer.

1. Flash Cards. Encourage your child to make his or her own sets of flash cards to review grammar points. (Making the cards as well as using them helps your child remember.) For example, some verbs in English must be followed by a gerund; others must be followed by an infinitive. One side of a flash card would have the verb (admit) and the other side would have an example with the gerund or the infinitive. (For example, "He admits losing the library book." *Losing* is a gerund.)

2. Possessions. Walk around your house with your child and ask about family members' belongings. Your child can answer using possessive adjectives (my, your, his, her, its, our, their) or possessive pronouns (mine, yours, his, hers, ours, theirs). For example, if you point at a briefcase, your child can say, "It's Daddy's. It's his briefcase." (or "It's his.") If you point at your child's bed, he or she will say, "That's my bed." (or "It's mine.")

3. Grammar Poster. Help your child make a self-correcting grammar poster. A poster for irregular plurals is a good example. Down the left side of the page would be a list of singular nouns. The correct irregular plural would be written in a center column, and the right side of the page would be folded over the answer column in the middle so that the answers are hidden. Your child would look at the singular noun (foot), say what he or she thinks is the correct irregular plural form (feet), and then check the answer by looking under the folded part of the poster paper.

NOTE: If you or other family members know English, do the activities in English with your child. If you do not, do them in your own language, and they will still help your child focus on concepts that will eventually build a better awareness of grammar.

Estimados padres de familia:

El propósito de aprender un nuevo idioma es poder comunicarnos claramente en ese idioma. Para tal fin es importante aprender las reglas gramaticales y saber usarlas correctamente. Usted puede darle a su hijo o hija la oportunidad de practicar inglés en la casa dedicando un rato a la semana a realizar actividades de gramática como las que se sugieren a continuación. Esta práctica adicional le ayudará a su hijo/a a ser un mejor orador, lector y escritor en inglés.

1. **Tarjetas de gramática.** Anime a su hijo/a a hacer su propio juego de tarjetas para revisar conceptos gramaticales. (El hacer y usar las tarjetas le ayuda a su hijo/a a recordar.) Por ejemplo, algunos verbos tanto en inglés como en español son seguidos por un gerundio; otros son seguidos por un infinitivo. Un lado de la tarjeta tendrá el verbo (espera) y el otro lado tendrá un ejemplo con el gerundio o infinitivo. (Por ejemplo, *El espera jugando*) *Jugando* es un gerundio.

2. **Posesivos.** Recorra la casa con su hijo/a haciéndole preguntas sobre las pertenencias de los miembros de la familia. Su hijo/a puede responder usando adjetivos posesivos *(mí, tu, su, nuestra)* o pronombres posesivos *(mío, tuyo, de él, de ella, nuestra, de ellos).* Por ejemplo, si usted señala un maletín, su hijo/a puede decir: "Es de papi. Es su maletín." Si usted señala la cama de su hijo/a, puede decir: "Es mi cama" o "Es mía".

3. **Cartel de gramática.** Ayude a su hijo/a a hacer un cartel de gramática con auto-correcciones. Un buen ejemplo es un cartel con plurales irregulares. Al lado izquierdo de la página habría una lista de sustantivos singulares. El plural irregular correcto estaría en la columna del centro y el lado derecho de la página estaría doblado cubriendo la columna de respuestas de la mitad. Su hijo/a lee el sustantivo singular *(mouse,* ratón), dice cuál cree que es el plural irregular correcto *(mice,* ratones), y después revisa la respuesta mirando la parte oculta del cartel.

NOTA: Si usted u otro miembro de la familia habla inglés, realice las actividades en inglés con su hijo/a. Si no sabe inglés, hágalas en su propio idioma porque de cualquier forma le ayudarán a su hijo/a a concentrarse en conceptos que le permitirán tener un mejor dominio gramatical.

Dear Parents,

All language learners use dictionaries, and it is important to know how to use one correctly. If possible, have a regular English dictionary as well as an English-native language dictionary in your home. Help your child become familiar with the different kinds of information dictionaries offer by sharing some of the activities below.

1. Picture Dictionary. For a young child, a picture dictionary is a fun and easy way to associate images and the words that name them. Have your child listen and point as you read aloud the different words that correspond to the pictures. Later, have him or her repeat the words and point. As a memory game, choose a page and cover up the words with slips of paper. Have your child tell you the words under the paper slips.

2. Word Hunt. Make a list of words beginning with different letters and have your child write down the page number of the dictionary on which he or she found each word. To increase the difficulty, set a time limit.

3. Holiday Words. Prepare a list of words related to different holidays. Then, on a piece of paper, have your child group the words according to the appropriate holidays. He or she will need to use the dictionary to find which holidays some of the words are associated with. For example, fireworks are associated with the Fourth of July and with New Year's Eve, carols and mistletoe with Christmas, and candles and gifts with birthdays.

4. Spellings. A good dictionary lists all the correct spelling possibilities for a word (often there is more than one spelling). Prepare a list of words and have your child find out how many spellings each word has and what they are. You may want him or her to fill in a chart with the following information: word, number of spellings, first spelling, second spelling, and so on.

NOTE: If you or other family members know English, do the activities in English with your child. If you do not, do them in your own language, and they will still help your child become more confident about understanding and using the different parts of the dictionary.

Estimados padres de familia:

Al aprender un nuevo idioma hay que saber usar el diccionario correctamente. Si es posible, tenga en casa un diccionario de inglés así como un diccionario de su lengua natal. Ayude a su hijo o hija a familiarizarse con los diferentes tipos de información que los diccionarios ofrecen realizando las siguientes actividades.

1. **Diccionario ilustrado.** Para un niño pequeño, un diccionario ilustrado es un modo divertido y fácil de asociar imágenes y palabras. Pida a su hijo/a que escuche y señale a medida que usted lee en voz alta las distintas palabras que corresponden a las ilustraciones. Más adelante, pídale que sea él o ella quien diga las palabras y las señale. Como un juego de memoria, elija una página y cubra las palabras con tiras de papel. Pida a su hijo/a que le diga las palabras que hay debajo de las tiras de papel.

2. **Cacería de palabras.** Haga una lista de palabras que comiencen con distintas letras y pida a su hijo/a que escriba el número de la página del diccionario en la que encontró cada palabra. Para aumentar el grado de dificultad, fije un límite de tiempo.

3. **Palabras festivas.** Prepare una lista de palabras relacionadas con distintos días festivos. Después, en una hoja de papel, pida a su hijo/a que agrupe las palabras según los días festivos apropiados. Tal vez deba usar el diccionario para buscar los días festivos vinculados a esas palabras. Por ejemplo, los fuegos artificiales están asociados con el Cuatro de Julio y con el Año Nuevo, los villancicos y las hojas de muérdago con la Navidad y las velitas y regalos con los cumpleaños.

4. **Deletrear palabras.** Un buen diccionario cita todas las formas correctas en que se puede deletrear una palabra (a menudo hay más de una forma). Prepare una lista de palabras y pida a su hijo/a que halle cuántas formas hay de deletrear cada palabra y cuáles son. Puede pedirle que complete una tabla con la siguiente información: palabra, en cuántas formas se puede deletrear, primera forma, segunda forma y así sucesivamente.

NOTA: Si usted u otro miembro de la familia habla inglés, realice las actividades en inglés con su hijo/a. Si no sabe inglés, hágalas en su propio idioma porque de cualquier forma le ayudarán a su hijo/a a entender y usar mejor las diferentes partes de un diccionario.

Dear Parents,

Dictionaries are a valuable tool for language learners. It is a good idea to have at least two dictionaries at home: a regular English dictionary and a native language-English dictionary. Dictionaries offer a variety of information as well as definitions of words, and it is important to know how to take advantage of all the help a good dictionary can provide. Sharing the activities below will help your child build confidence and skill in dictionary use.

1. Parts of Speech. A good dictionary indicates what part of speech a word is by using abbreviations such as n (noun), v (verb), adj (adjective), and prep (preposition). Prepare a varied list of words and have your child use the dictionary to find out what part of speech each one is (some words can be more than one part of speech).

2. Stress. Good dictionaries give information about pronunciation. When a word has more than one syllable, one of those syllables receives stress (greater force or emphasis) when it is pronounced. Look in the dictionary with your child to see how the stress of a word is identified in your dictionary (there are several methods). Then give your child a list of multisyllable words to look up. Have him or her mark the stress of each word.

3. Guess Ahead. Prepare a list of ten to fifteen words, some of which are words you have invented (not real words; for example *glippery, snubble, fryous,* and *slank*). Have your child look at the list and guess which words are made up and which words are real. Then have him or her look up each of the words to find out. Have him or her write down the page number where he or she found each word; the invented words, of course, will not be in the dictionary.

4. In Order. Make a list of words beginning with the same letter and then have your child list them in the order in which they appear in the dictionary. For example, if you give him or her *pay, pain, pie, pawn, pea,* and *payoff,* the order in which they appear in the dictionary is *pain, pawn, pay, payoff, pea,* and *pie.* For a challenge, set a time limit.

NOTE: If you or other family members know English, do the activities in English with your child. If you do not, do them in your own language, and they will still help your child become more confident about understanding and using the different parts of the dictionary.

Estimados padres de familia:

Los diccionarios son valiosas herramientas en el aprendizaje de un idioma. Es conveniente tener por lo menos dos diccionarios en la casa: un diccionario regular de inglés y un diccionario de su lengua natal. Los diccionarios ofrecen mucha información así como definición de palabras. Es importante saber aprovechar toda la ayuda que un buen diccionario brinda. El hacer las siguientes actividades puede ayudarle a su hijo/a a saber usar un diccionario con mayor seguridad.

1. Partes de la oración. Un buen diccionario indica qué función cumple una palabra en una oración usando una abreviatura como s. (sustantivo), v. (verbo), adj. (adjetivo) y prep. (preposición). Prepare una lista variada de palabras y pida a su hijo/a que use el diccionario para hallar qué parte de la oración es cada palabra (algunas palabras pueden ser más de una parte de la oración).

2. Énfasis. Los buenos diccionarios dan información acerca de la pronunciación. Cuando una palabra tiene más de una sílaba, una de esas sílabas recibe el énfasis (mayor fuerza) cuando se pronuncia. Revisen con su hijo/a el diccionario para ver cómo se identifica el énfasis de una palabra en su diccionario (hay varios métodos). Después, dé a su hijo/a una lista de palabras con varias sílabas para buscar en el diccionario. Pídale que marque el énfasis en cada palabra.

3. Adivínalo. Prepare una lista de diez a quince palabras, algunas de las cuales son inventadas por usted (palabras que no existen como *gluta, solte, frano* y *sertal).* Pida a su hijo/a que mire la lista y adivine qué palabras son inventadas y qué palabras son reales. Después pídale que busque en el diccionario cada una de las palabras. Pídale que escriba el número de la página donde encontró cada palabra. Las palabras inventadas, obviamente, no aparecerán en el diccionario.

4. En orden. Haga una lista de palabras que comiencen con la misma letra y después pídale a su hijo/a que las escriba en una lista siguiendo el orden del diccionario. Por ejemplo, si usted le da una lista con las palabras *pagar, portal, pie, paño, pera* y *pastor,* el orden en que aparecen en el diccionario es *pagar, paño, pastor, pera, pie* y *portal.* Para que el reto sea mayor, fije un límite de tiempo.

NOTA: Si usted u otro miembro de la familia habla inglés, realice las actividades en inglés con su hijo/a. Si no sabe inglés, hágalas en su propio idioma porque de cualquier forma le ayudarán a su hijo/a a entender y usar mejor las diferentes partes de un diccionario.

Dear Parents,

Successful readers and writers know how to take advantage of the many kinds of information a good dictionary provides. As an English-language learner, your child will benefit from additional practice using the dictionary. You can help your child build his or her dictionary skills at home by spending a few minutes a week doing the activities suggested below.

1. Guide Words. Guide words are found in the top left-hand corner and top right-hand corner of a dictionary page or two-page spread. The left-hand word is the first word entry on the page, and the right-hand word is the last word entry on that page. Looking at these words helps you know if the word you want is on that page. Help your child become familiar with using guide words by preparing a few questions for him or her to answer. For example, list the guide words on three consecutive pages and then ask your child where he or she will find a particular word. You may say, "Where can you find the word *funds:* between the guide words *frugal* and *fun, function* and *fuss,* or *futile* and *gambit?*"

2. Sound-Alikes. In English, the same sound can have different spellings. Give your child this list of words and ask him or her to use the dictionary to find out if the words have the same or similar pronunciation or not. For example, meat/mete (yes); bead/dead (no); *under/wonder* (yes); cents/sense (yes); though/thought (no); know/no (yes); seed/cede (yes); cater/water (no); and bough/how (yes).

3. Abbreviations. Have your child use the dictionary to find and write out the complete form of each of these abbreviations: AM, COD, RSVP, ASAP, INC, GA, www, CD, mm, and TSP. On another day, provide complete expressions and have your child look up the abbreviations.

NOTE: If you or other family members know English, do the activities in English with your child. If you do not, do them in your own language, and they will still help your child become more confident about understanding and using the different parts of the dictionary.

Estimados padres de familia:

Los buenos lectores y escritores saben aprovechar los muchos tipos de información que brinda un buen diccionario. En su aprendizaje del inglés, su hijo o hija se beneficiará de la práctica adicional para usar un diccionario. Para ayudarle en la casa a desarrollar estas destrezas, dediquen unos pocos minutos a la semana a hacer las siguientes actividades.

1. Palabras-guía. Las palabras-guía se encuentran en la esquina superior izquierda y en la esquina superior derecha de la página individual o de la doble página de un diccionario. La palabra que aparece en la esquina de la izquierda es la primera palabra de la página y la palabra que aparece en la esquina de la derecha es la última palabra de esa página. Estas palabras ayudan a saber si la palabra que se busca está en la página. Ayude a su hijo/a a familiarizarse con el uso de las palabras-guía preparando unas cuantas preguntas para que las responda. Por ejemplo, diga las palabras-guía en tres páginas consecutivas y después pregúntele a su hijo/a dónde puede encontrar una palabra en particular. Usted podría decir: "¿Dónde puedes encontrar la palabra *foca:* entre las palabras-guía *fluir* y *fogata,* o entre *fósforo* y *fomento,* o entre *futuro* y *gacela?*

2. Sonidos similares. En inglés, el mismo sonido se puede deletrear de distinto modo. Dé a su hijo/a una lista de palabras y pídale que use el diccionario para averiguar si las palabras tienen o no tienen una pronunciación igual o similar. Por ejemplo, meat/mete (sí); bead/dead (no); *under/wonder* (sí); cents/sense (sí); though/thought (no); Know/no (sí); seed/cede (sí); cater/water (no); y bough/how (sí).

3. Abreviatura. Pida a su hijo/a que use el diccionario para averiguar y escribir la forma completa de cada una de estas abreviaturas: AM, COD, RSVP, ASAP, INC, GA, www, CD, mm y TSP. Otro día, puede darle la expresión completa y pedirle que busque las abreviaturas.

NOTA: Si usted u otro miembro de la familia habla inglés, realice las actividades en inglés con su hijo/a. Si no sabe inglés, hágalas en su propio idioma porque de cualquier forma le ayudarán a su hijo/a a entender y usar mejor las diferentes partes de un diccionario.

Dear Parents,

Your child is learning English, and like all language learners, he or she needs to become familiar with the different types of information a good dictionary offers. Good dictionary skills will help your child become a more efficient reader and writer. As parents, you can provide your child with additional opportunities to practice these skills through sharing the activities below.

1. Extras. Many dictionaries provide additional kinds of information. Help your child become aware of the extra features your dictionary has by making a checklist and having your child check yes or no. Ask about the following features: a table of common measurements, a list of common male and female names, a pronunciation table, a summary of grammar rules, a key to the codes and abbreviations used in the dictionary, maps, inclusion of historical names such as Aristotle or Napoleon, illustrations, spelling rules, a list of irregular verbs, explanations of the origins of words, and so on.

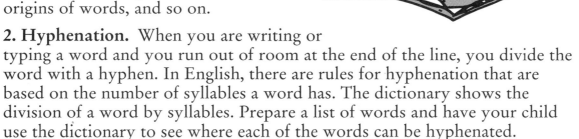

2. Hyphenation. When you are writing or typing a word and you run out of room at the end of the line, you divide the word with a hyphen. In English, there are rules for hyphenation that are based on the number of syllables a word has. The dictionary shows the division of a word by syllables. Prepare a list of words and have your child use the dictionary to see where each of the words can be hyphenated.

3. Usage Labels. In any language, some words are more formal than others. It is important to know when it is correct to use a certain word. Most dictionaries use labels such as formal, informal, spoken, slang, and offensive. Prepare a list of words and have your child use the dictionary to find out when it is appropriate to use each of the words. For example, you may ask about *bucks, madam, geek, affirm, gonna, dine, chow, incarcerate, whiz, zit, airhead, in lieu of,* and *slob.*

NOTE: If you or other family members know English, do the activities in English with your child. If you do not, do them in your own language, and they will still help your child become more confident about understanding and using the different parts of the dictionary.

Estimados padres de familia:

Su hijo o hija está aprendiendo inglés, y cómo todo el que aprende un idioma, necesita familiarizarse con los diferentes tipos de información que ofrece un buen diccionario. Las destrezas para usar el diccionario le ayudarán a su hijo o hija a ser un lector y escritor más eficiente. Como padres, ustedes pueden brindarle oportunidades de practicar estas destrezas realizando las siguientes actividades.

1. Información adicional. Muchos diccionarios ofrecen tipos de información adicional. Para ayudar a su hijo/a a reconocer las características adicionales que tiene su diccionario, haga una lista y pídale a su hijo/a que marque sí o no. Pregunte si tiene las siguientes características: una lista de pesos y medidas usuales, una lista de nombres masculinos y femeninos comunes, una tabla de pronunciación, un resumen de reglas gramaticales, una lista de claves de los códigos y abreviaturas que se usan en el diccionario, mapas, inclusión de nombres históricos como Aristóteles o Napoleón, ilustraciones, reglas de ortografía, una lista de verbos irregulares, explicación del origen de las palabras y así sucesivamente.

2. División de palabras. Cuando se escribe a mano o a máquina y falta espacio al final del renglón, se divide la palabra con un guión. En inglés, hay reglas para dividir la palabra basándose en el número de sílabas que tiene una palabra. El diccionario muestra la división de una palabra por sílabas. Prepare una lista de palabras y pida a su hijo/a que use el diccionario para ver en qué partes se puede dividir cada una de las palabras.

3. Usos. En cualquier idioma hay palabras más formales que otras. Es importante saber cuando es correcto usar cierta palabra. La mayoría de diccionarios usan títulos como formal, informal, coloquial, jerga y ofensivo. Prepare una lista de palabras y pida a su hijo/a que use el diccionario para buscar cuándo es apropiado usar cada palabra.

Por ejemplo, puede pedirle que busque las palabras *bucks, madam, geek, affirm, gonna, dine, chow, incarcerate, whiz, zit, airhead, in lieu of* y *slob.*

NOTA: Si usted u otro miembro de la familia habla inglés, realice las actividades en inglés con su hijo/a. Si no sabe inglés, hágalas en su propio idioma porque de cualquier forma le ayudarán a su hijo/a a entender y usar mejor las diferentes partes de un diccionario.

Dear Parents,

Successful students use a variety of strategies called critical thinking skills. These skills result in more effective learning and in a more self-confident, independent learner. Examples of these skills and strategies include classifying, sequencing, making inferences, drawing conclusions, using graphics, and applying prior knowledge. As parents, you can help your child practice using thinking skills and learning strategies that will aid him or her in the classroom and in later life.

1. Classifying. Provide your child with a box full of different items or a big pile of pictures. Have him or her sort them into groups based on categories that either of you provide. For example, you might have your child sort clothes according to the appropriate season, toys according to their owners, sports equipment according to the appropriate sport, kitchen items according to size, pictures of places according to the appropriate continent, characters in a story or TV program as major or minor, countries on a map as wealthy or developing, family members and relatives according to age, and so on.

2. Similarities and Differences. Help your child make a list or chart to identify similarities and differences between two items. For example, on one side of a page, he or she could list similarities between dogs and cats, and on the other side of the page differences between dogs and cats. Have your child make a chart about family members, favorite TV programs, cars and trucks, TVs and computers, soccer and basketball, fruits and vegetables.

3. In Sequence. Challenge your child to perform a task such as making a sandwich or turning on the computer and opening a file by saying or writing each specific step in the correct sequence. Encourage him or her to use sequence words such as *first, second, next, during, after,* and so on. To encourage awareness of sequence in written text, provide your child with a joke or story cut up into strips that he or she must reassemble in logical sequence.

NOTE: If you or other family members speak English, do the activities in English with your child. If you do not, do them in your own language, and they will still help your child focus on strategies that will eventually transfer to his or her English language-learning experience.

Estimados padres de familia:

Los buenos estudiantes usan una serie de estrategias llamadas destrezas de pensamiento crítico. Estas destrezas promueven un aprendizaje más efectivo y mayor confianza e independencia. Entre estas destrezas figuran clasificar, formar secuencias, hacer inferencias, sacar conclusiones, usar gráficas y aplicar conocimientos previos. Como padres, ustedes pueden ayudarle a su hijo/a a practicar el uso de destrezas de pensamiento y aprendizaje que le ayudarán en el salón de clase y en su vida futura.

1. Clasificar. Entregue a su hijo/a una caja llena de diferentes objetos o un montón grande de ilustraciones. Pídale que los clasifique en grupos basándose en categorías sugeridas por alguno de los dos. Por ejemplo, puede pedirle a su hijo/a que clasifique ropa según la estación apropiada, juguetes según sus dueños, equipo deportivo según cada deporte, utensilios de cocina según el tamaño, ilustraciones de lugares según el continente

apropiado, personajes de un cuento o de un programa de televisión como principales o secundarios, países en un mapa como ricos o en desarrollo, miembros de la familia y parientes según su edad, y así sucesivamente.

2. Similitudes y diferencias. Ayude a su hijo/a a hacer una lista o tabla para identificar similitudes y diferencias entre dos objetos. Por ejemplo, en un lado de la página puede hacer una lista de similitudes entre perros y gatos y en el otro lado puede hacer una lista de diferencias entre perros y gatos. Pídale a su hijo/a que haga una tabla acerca de miembros de la familia, programas de televisión favoritos, autos y camiones, televisores y computadoras, fútbol y baloncesto, frutas y vegetales.

3. En secuencia. Rete a su hijo/a a realizar una tarea tal como hacer un sándwich o prender la computadora y abrir un archivo diciendo o escribiendo cada paso específico en la secuencia correcta. Anímelo/a a usar palabras de secuencia tales como *primero, después, durante, después de* y así sucesivamente. Para afianzar la noción de la secuencia en un texto escrito, dé a su hijo/a un chiste o cuento cortado en tiras para que lo vuelva a ordenar en su secuencia lógica.

NOTA: Si usted u otro miembro de la familia habla inglés, realice las actividades en inglés con su hijo/a. Si no sabe inglés, hágalas en su propio idioma porque de cualquier forma le ayudarán a su hijo/a a concentrarse en estrategias que le servirán para el aprendizaje del inglés.

Dear Parents,

As parents, you want your child to succeed both in school and in later life. One way to help him or her become a more efficient English-language learner is to provide opportunities for practice at home. Good learners use different strategies and skills such as making inferences, using graphics, associating, and predicting as they study. You can help your child get additional practice in these critical thinking skills by sharing the activities below.

1. Predicting. Good readers and listeners pay attention to details that help them predict what will come next in a text or conversation. When your child reads, have him or her look at titles, captions, and illustrations to predict what the story or text will be about. When you are talking with your child, say sentences such as "I had a great day at work" or "Let's go out this weekend," and then ask him or her to predict what might come next. Your child could say, "You'll tell me all about the good things that happened at work today" or "You'll suggest some places we could go."

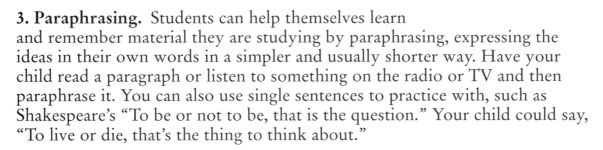

2. Using Graphics. Help your child become familiar with maps, charts, and graphs in newspapers and magazines. For example, you may look at the weather page in the newspaper together and have him or her tell you about weather conditions using the weather charts, symbols, and maps. The sports section of the newspaper often has charts, statistics, and so on as well.

3. Paraphrasing. Students can help themselves learn and remember material they are studying by paraphrasing, expressing the ideas in their own words in a simpler and usually shorter way. Have your child read a paragraph or listen to something on the radio or TV and then paraphrase it. You can also use single sentences to practice with, such as Shakespeare's "To be or not to be, that is the question." Your child could say, "To live or die, that's the thing to think about."

NOTE: If you or other family members speak English, do the activities in English with your child. If you do not, do them in your own language, and they will still help your child focus on strategies that will eventually transfer to his or her English language-learning experience.

Estimados padres de familia:

Como padres, ustedes desean que su hijo o hija triunfe tanto en la escuela como en su vida futura. Un modo de ayudarle a aprender el inglés de modo más eficiente es darle oportunidades de practicar en casa. Los buenos estudiantes usan varias estrategias y destrezas tales como hacer inferencias, usar gráficas, asociar y hacer predicciones. Ustedes pueden ayudarle a su hijo/a a practicar estas destrezas de pensamiento crítico compartiendo las siguientes actividades.

1. Predecir. Los buenos lectores y oyentes prestan atención a detalles que les ayudan a predecir lo que vendrá después en un texto o conversación. Cuando su hijo/a lea, pídale que mire los títulos, leyendas de fotos e ilustraciones para predecir de qué será el cuento o texto. Cuando usted hable con su hijo/a, diga oraciones tales como "Hoy tuve un excelente día en el trabajo" "Vamos a salir este fin de semana" y después pídale que prediga qué vendrá después. Su hijo/a podría decir: "Me vas a contar todo lo bueno que te pasó hoy en el trabajo" o "Vas a decir a dónde podemos ir".

2. Usar gráficas. Ayude a su hijo/a a familiarizarse con mapas, tablas y gráficas en periódicos y revistas. Por ejemplo, pueden mirar juntos la página del clima en el periódico y pedirle que le hable acerca de las condiciones del tiempo usando las tablas del clima, los símbolos y mapas. La sección deportiva del periódico a menudo tiene tablas, estadísticas y cosas por el estilo.

3. Parafrasear. Para aprender y recordar mejor los materiales de estudio, los estudiantes pueden parafrasear, es decir expresar las ideas en sus propias palabras de un modo más simple y corto. Pida a su hijo/a que lea un párrafo o que escuche algo por radio o televisión para luego parafrasearlo. También puede darle oraciones individuales para practicar, tales como la famosa de Shakespeare "Ser o no ser, ésa es la pregunta". Su hijo/a podría parafrasear diciendo: "Vivir o morir, eso es en lo que hay que pensar".

NOTA: Si usted u otro miembro de la familia habla inglés, realice las actividades en inglés con su hijo/a. Si no sabe inglés, hágalas en su propio idioma porque de cualquier forma le ayudarán a su hijo/a a concentrarse en estrategias que le servirán para el aprendizaje del inglés.

Dear Parents,

Critical thinking skills are a group of strategies that students can use to become more effective learners. Some of these activities include brainstorming, classifying, associating, and making inferences. You can provide your child with additional opportunities to practice these valuable skills at home by sharing the suggestions below. Your child can become a more self-confident and independent learner with your help.

1. Ranking. Help your child become familiar with the concept of ranking. Have him or her rank different items in order of preference, importance, height, price, and so on. Begin by having your child rank his or her top ten toys in order of preference (#1 = most favorite, #10 = least favorite). Then have him or her list his or her favorite foods, sports, books, TV shows, songs, and so on.

2. Memory Helps. Talk about the little memory tricks people use to remember facts and details. Give an example or two from your own culture. Then show your child these two examples in English. To remember the colors of the rainbow in order, people use the name ROY G. BIV (each letter corresponds to a color in the rainbow: red, orange, yellow, green, blue, indigo, violet). To remember the word *zipper*, students think of the /z/ sound a zipper makes as it opens or closes. Encourage your child to think of others.

3. Cause and Effect. Help your child see the relationship between cause and effect in English by focusing on words such as *why, because, therefore, as a result, since, due to, for this reason,* and *so*. Have him or her identify these words in paragraphs and explain the cause-effect relationships to which they refer. For speaking practice with younger children, ask questions such as "Why did the dinosaurs disappear?" or "Why do we carry umbrellas?" Your child may say, "Because the climate changed" or "So we won't get wet."

NOTE: If you or other family members speak English, do the activities in English with your child. If you do not, do them in your own language, and they will still help your child focus on strategies that will eventually transfer to his or her English language-learning experience.

Estimados padres de familia:

Las destrezas de pensamiento crítico son un grupo de estrategias que los estudiantes pueden usar para un aprendizaje más efectivo. Algunas de estas actividades incluyen idear, clasificar, asociar y hacer inferencias. Para darle a su hijo o hija oportunidades adicionales de practicar estas valiosas destrezas en casa, puede hacer las actividades que se sugieren a continuación. Con su ayuda, su hijo/a podrá aprender con mayor confianza e independencia.

1. Clasificar. Ayude a su hijo/a a familiarizarse con el concepto de clasificación. Pídale que clasifique diferentes objetos en orden de preferencia, importancia, altura, precio y así sucesivamente. Comience por pedirle que clasifique sus primeros diez juguetes en orden de preferencia (# 1 = el preferido, # 10 = el menos preferido), alimentos, deportes, libros, programas de televisión, canciones, etc.

2. Trucos para memorizar. Hable de los pequeños trucos que la gente usa para recordar hechos y detalles. Dé uno o dos ejemplos de su propia cultura. Después muéstrele a su hijo/a estos dos ejemplos en inglés. Para recordar los colores del arco iris en orden, la gente usa en inglés el nombre ROY G. BIV (cada letra corresponde a un color del arco iris: *red*/rojo *orange*/naranja 3/amarillo, *green*/verde, *blue*/azul, *indigo*/añil, *violet*/violeta). Para recordar la palabra *zipper,* los estudiantes piensan en el sonido de la /z/ que una cremallera hace al abrirse y cerrarse. Anime a su hijo/a a pensar en otros ejemplos.

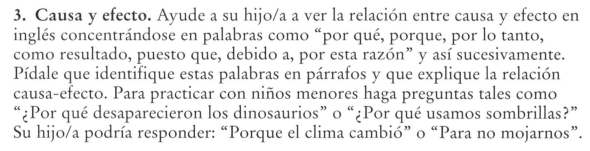

3. Causa y efecto. Ayude a su hijo/a a ver la relación entre causa y efecto en inglés concentrándose en palabras como "por qué, porque, por lo tanto, como resultado, puesto que, debido a, por esta razón" y así sucesivamente. Pídale que identifique estas palabras en párrafos y que explique la relación causa-efecto. Para practicar con niños menores haga preguntas tales como "¿Por qué desaparecieron los dinosaurios" o "¿Por qué usamos sombrillas?" Su hijo/a podría responder: "Porque el clima cambió" o "Para no mojarnos".

NOTA: Si usted u otro miembro de la familia habla inglés, realice las actividades en inglés con su hijo/a. Si no sabe inglés, hágalas en su propio idioma porque de cualquier forma le ayudarán a su hijo/a a concentrarse en estrategias que le servirán para el aprendizaje del inglés.

Dear Parents,

In the classroom and in later life, critical thinking skills and strategies play an important part in successful learning. Activities such as using charts and graphs, brainstorming, making inferences, and classifying help students become more independent and creative learners. You can help your child become a more efficient English-language learner through spending some time each week doing the activities suggested below.

1. Making Associations. Associating groups of words or ideas helps in learning and remembering them. If your child has vocabulary lists of words to learn or review, help him or her make meaningful associations with them instead of trying to memorize an alphabetized list of random words. For example, in a long list of words, there may be several that can be associated because they are all found in a house, or because they all have to do with travel and vacations, or because they all relate to crime in some way. Logical associations such as the above are not the only kind people make. Your child might group words together because he or she likes the way they sound or the way they look. Encourage your child to make associations often.

2. Making Inferences. When information we want is not directly stated in a text or conversation, we focus on words related to the information we want to help us make a decision or come to a conclusion. Help your child practice making inferences by describing simple situations, such as "A boy has a torn shirt. His hair is messed up. His face is red, and he has a bruise on his face. His cheeks are wet." Your child would say, "The boy has been in a fight." When reading with your child, have him or her make inferences about the characters in the story. For example, if a character is always alone in his house, always looking out the window, always playing sad music, always checking an empty mailbox, your child could say, "He is very lonely and unhappy" or "His girlfriend left him."

NOTE: If you or other family members speak English, do the activities in English with your child. If you do not, do them in your own language, and they will still help your child focus on strategies that will eventually transfer to his or her English language-learning experience.

Estimados padres de familia:

Tanto en el salón de clase como en la vida futura, las destrezas y estrategias de pensamiento crítico son parte importante del aprendizaje. Actividades tales como usar tablas y gráficas, idear, hacer inferencias y clasificar, ayudan a los estudiantes a ser más independientes y creativos. Ustedes pueden ayudarle a su hijo o hija a aprender inglés de modo más efectivo dedicando un rato de cada semana a hacer las siguientes actividades.

1. Hacer asociaciones. Para aprender y recordar palabras o ideas, es útil asociarlas en grupos. Si su hijo/a lleva a la casa listas de vocabulario o de palabras para aprender y repasar, ayúdele a hacer asociaciones lógicas en lugar de tratar de memorizar una lista alfabetizada de palabras por aparte. Por ejemplo, en una lista larga de palabras, puede haber varias que se pueden asociar por encontrarse en una casa o porque tienen que ver con viajes o vacaciones, o porque tienen

alguna relación con el crimen. Pero éstas no son las únicas asociaciones lógicas que se pueden hacer. Su hijo/a puede agrupar palabras porque le gusta el sonido que hacen o el modo en que se ven. Anime a su hijo/a a hacer asociaciones a menudo.

2. Hacer inferencias. Cuando la información que queremos no se establece directamente en un texto o conversación, nos concentramos en palabras relacionadas con la información que necesitamos para poder tomar una decisión o llegar a una conclusión. Ayude a su hijo/a a practicar la destreza de hacer inferencias describiendo situaciones simples tales como "Un chico llega a la casa con la ropa rasgada, despeinado y con la cara colorada y llena de golpes. Tiene las mejillas húmedas". Su hijo podría decir: "El chico estuvo en una pelea". Al leer con su hijo/a, pídale que haga inferencias acerca de los personajes del cuento. Por ejemplo, si un personaje siempre está solo en su casa, mira por la ventaja, oye música triste y abre el buzón del correo con frecuencia, su hijo podría decir: "Está muy solo y triste" o "Su novia lo dejó".

NOTA: Si usted u otro miembro de la familia habla inglés, realice las actividades en inglés con su hijo/a. Si no sabe inglés, hágalas en su propio idioma porque de cualquier forma le ayudarán a su hijo/a a concentrarse en estrategias que le servirán para el aprendizaje del inglés.

Dear Parents:

At school, your child learns social and cultural behaviors as well as English and other subjects. Appropriate social behaviors and sensitivity to different cultures are very important. You can help your child feel more confident and comfortable at school in several ways. You can talk about his own country, traditions, and heritage and encourage him or her to feel proud of who he or she is. At the same time, you can help your child adjust to any feelings of discomfort, fear, or difference that he or she may experience at school.

1. The American Way. Help your child understand that his or her teachers may expect behaviors that may surprise or confuse him or her. For example, teachers expect students to express their own opinions, ask questions when they are confused, and volunteer for classroom activities. Teachers often allow informal behavior and may permit students to disagree with them. They expect students to have direct eye contact with them every few seconds and raise their hands to volunteer answers to any question they may ask. (A very quiet child who never looks teachers in the eye as a sign of respect may be considered lazy or even indifferent to what is going on in the classroom.) Children are often encouraged to work with partners or in a group as well, and sometimes even share in a group grade for an activity.

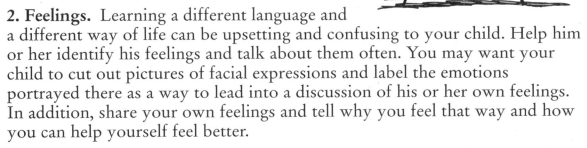

2. Feelings. Learning a different language and a different way of life can be upsetting and confusing to your child. Help him or her identify his feelings and talk about them often. You may want your child to cut out pictures of facial expressions and label the emotions portrayed there as a way to lead into a discussion of his or her own feelings. In addition, share your own feelings and tell why you feel that way and how you can help yourself feel better.

3. "If" Cards. To help your child identify and choose correct behaviors for social/cultural situations, play this "What If" game. On one side of a series of index cards, write out situations such as "Someone takes your favorite toy/There is a fire in the next house/Someone says you should go back to your country," and so on. Discuss feelings and appropriate behaviors for each.

NOTE: If you or other family members speak English, do the activities in English with your child. If you do not, do them in your own language, and they will still help your child develop socially and culturally in a way that will eventually help his or her transition in the American classroom.

Estimados padres de familia:

Su hijo o hija está aprendiendo conductas sociales y culturales en la escuela junto con inglés y otras asignaturas. Es muy importante tener una conducta social apropiada y ser sensible a otras culturas. Hay muchos modos en que puede ayudar a su hijo/a a sentirse más seguro y cómodo en la escuela. Puede hablarle acerca de su propio país, de sus tradiciones y herencias, y estimularlo a sentir orgullo de su origen. Al mismo tiempo, usted puede ayudarle a ajustarse a las emociones de inquietud, miedo o sensación de ser diferente que pueda experimentar en la escuela.

1. Costumbres americanas. Ayude a su hijo/a a entender que sus maestros esperan que se comporte de un modo que tal vez le sorprenda o confunda. Por ejemplo, los maestros esperan que los estudiantes expresen sus propias opiniones, que hagan preguntas cuando están confundidos y que se ofrezcan como voluntarios para las actividades del salón de clase. Los maestros a menudo aceptan una conducta informal y permiten que los estudiantes manifiesten su desacuerdo. Esperan que los estudiantes los miren directamente a los ojos y que levanten la mano si quieren contestar una pregunta.  (Un niño muy callado que nunca mira a los maestros a los ojos como signo de respeto, puede ser considerado perezoso o incluso indiferente a lo que está pasando en el salón de clase.) A menudo se anima a los niños a que trabajen con compañeros o en un grupo para una actividad.

2. Sentimientos. El aprender otro idioma y un estilo diferente de vida puede inquietar y confundir a un niño. Ayude a su hijo/a a identificar sus sentimientos y hablar de ellos a menudo. Puede pedirle que corte ilustraciones de expresiones faciales y que rotule las emociones que se muestran en la ilustración como un modo de promover una charla sobre sus propios sentimientos. Además, cuéntele sus propios sentimientos y dígale por qué se siente así y qué hace para sentirse mejor.

3. Suposiciones. Para ayudar a su hijo/a a identificar y elegir comportamientos correctos en situaciones socio/culturales, invítelo a jugar a las suposiciones. En un lado de una serie de tarjetas, escriba situaciones tales como "Alguien te quita tu juguete favorito/Hay un incendio en la casa de al lado/Te dicen que puedes regresar a tu país" y así sucesivamente. Comente los sentimientos y los comportamientos adecuados en cada caso.

NOTA: Si usted u otro miembro de la familia habla inglés, realice las actividades en inglés con su hijo/a. Si no sabe inglés, hágalas en su propio idioma porque de cualquier forma le ayudarán a su hijo/a en su desarrollo socio/cultural y facilitarán su transición al salón de clase estadounidense.

Dear Parents,

Children learn many things at school in addition to English and math. They learn how to play together, how to make friends, and how to act in different situations. As parents, you want your child to feel comfortable and happy at school so that he or she can do well. You can talk about living in and adjusting to a new culture and a new language with your child and review appropriate behaviors by sharing the activities below.

1. Self-Esteem. It is common for "newcomers" to feel unsure of themselves. A new child in the classroom may feel ugly, stupid, very shy, or angry. Make sure your child knows that he or she is loved and very special. Ask him or her about school and about his or her feelings every day. Find something positive to say to your child every day and offer support and encouragement. Mention how proud you are of his or her efforts.

2. Making Friends. Research shows that children who have a lot of friends and playmates are sensitive to changes in facial expressions and body language. Help your child become aware of different facial expressions, gestures, and even tone of voice. This is particularly important when these expressions and gestures have different meanings in other cultures. Look at pictures of people and at people on TV together. Ask your child how each person is feeling and how he or she can tell. Point out clues to look for.

3. Differences Are OK. Help your child understand that people from different cultures often have different habits, likes and dislikes, customs, and beliefs. A simple way to introduce this idea is to contrast how different cultures celebrate (or ignore) birthdays or to contrast what different cultures eat for breakfast. You might want your child to make a chart showing these differences. Let him or her know that differences are interesting, not bad.

NOTE: If you or other family members speak English, do the activities in English with your child. If you do not, do them in your own language, and they will still help your child develop socially and culturally in a way that will eventually help his or her transition in the American classroom.

Estimados padres de familia:

Los niños aprenden muchas cosas en la escuela además de inglés y matemáticas. Aprenden a jugar juntos, a hacer amigos y a actuar en distintas situaciones. Como padres, ustedes desean que su hijo o hija se sienta cómodo y feliz en la escuela para que pueda desempeñarse bien. Hable con su hijo/a acerca de lo que es vivir y ajustarse a una nueva cultura y a un nuevo idioma, y refuerce un comportamiento apropiado con las siguientes actividades.

1. Autoestima. Es muy común que los "recién llegados" se sientan inseguros de sí mismos. Un niño nuevo en un salón de clase puede sentirse feo, tonto, muy tímido o resentido. Asegúrese de que su hijo/a se sienta amado y muy especial. Pregúntele acerca de la escuela y acerca de sus sentimientos diarios. Trate de decirle algo positivo cada día y ofrézcale apoyo y ánimo. Dígale lo orgulloso/a que se siente de sus esfuerzos.

2. Nuevos amigos. Las investigaciones demuestran que los niños que tienen muchos amigos y compañeros de juego son sensibles a los cambios en las expresiones faciales y el lenguaje corporal. Ayude a su hijo/a a ser consciente de las distintas expresiones faciales, gestos e incluso tonos de voz. Esto es particularmente importante cuando estas expresiones y gestos tienen distintos significados en otras culturas. Vean juntos fotos de personas o personajes de televisión.
Pregunte a su hijo/a cómo se siente cada persona y cómo lo sabe. Señale qué claves hay que tener en cuenta para saberlo.

3. Se puede ser diferente. Ayude a su hijo/a a entender que la gente de diversas culturas a menudo tiene distintos hábitos, gustos, aversiones, costumbres y creencias. Un modo simple de presentar esta idea es contrastar cómo diversas culturas celebran (o ignoran) los cumpleaños o qué comen al desayuno. Su hijo/a podría hacer una tabla mostrando esas diferencias. Hágale ver que las diferencias son interesantes, no malas.

NOTA: Si usted u otro miembro de la familia habla inglés, realice las actividades en inglés con su hijo/a. Si no sabe inglés, hágalas en su propio idioma porque de cualquier forma le ayudarán a su hijo/a en su desarrollo socio/cultural y facilitarán su transición al salón de clase estadounidense.

Dear Parents,

Helping your child to adjust to a new culture and to a new language will make his or her classroom time a more comfortable experience. In a time of change, it is important to support your child emotionally. Be especially aware of his or her feelings and behaviors; have extra patience if necessary. Help your child build self-esteem and confidence by sharing the activities below.

1. Scrapbook. Your child may enjoy a "transition" scrapbook of photos, postcards, and letters from his or her old friends, together with photos of his or her new school, new home, new friends, postcards of the new town, and so on. Encourage your child to keep in touch with his or her past life by sending postcards and putting any replies in the scrapbook.

2. By Myself. Children in the United States have more independence than the children of some other cultures do. For example, they often have a voice in family decisions, choose their own clothes, walk to school or catch the bus by themselves, and so on. Observe the level of independence your child's classmates have and gradually allow him or her to make some decisions on his or her own and do what the other children do. Talk to your child about the responsibilities that go along with having some independence.

3. The Library. Get a free library card for your child from the local public library. Libraries are wonderful sources of social and cultural information, providing much more than books for your child to read. They often have story hours for children on weekends where your child can meet new friends and practice English in an atmosphere different from that of the classroom. They also show children's films and videos and sometimes have special craft workshops for children to enjoy.

NOTE: If you or other family members speak English, do the activities in English with your child. If you do not, do them in your own language, and they will still help your child develop socially and culturally in a way that will eventually help his or her transition in the American classroom.

Estimados padres de familia:

El ayudar a su hijo o hija a ajustarse a una nueva cultura y a un nuevo idioma hará que su experiencia en el salón de clase sea más fácil. Durante una época de cambios, es importante apoyar a su hijo/a emocionalmente. Tenga muy en cuenta sus sentimientos y comportamientos; sea más paciente si es necesario. Ayúdele a adquirir autoestima y confianza realizando estas actividades.

1. Album de recortes. A su hijo/a le puede gustar tener un álbum de "transición" con fotos, tarjetas postales y cartas de sus viejos amigos, junto con fotos de su nueva escuela, su nueva casa, sus nuevos amigos, tarjetas postales de su nueva ciudad y cosas por el estilo. Anime a su hijo/a a estar en contacto con su vida pasada enviando tarjetas postales y colocando cualquier respuesta en el álbum de recortes.

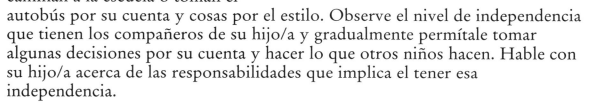

2. Por mi cuenta. Los niños en los Estados Unidos tienen más independencia que los de otras culturas. Por ejemplo, a menudo pueden opinar en una decisión familiar, eligen su propia ropa, caminan a la escuela o toman el autobús por su cuenta y cosas por el estilo. Observe el nivel de independencia que tienen los compañeros de su hijo/a y gradualmente permítale tomar algunas decisiones por su cuenta y hacer lo que otros niños hacen. Hable con su hijo/a acerca de las responsabilidades que implica el tener esa independencia.

3. En la biblioteca. Obtenga una tarjeta gratis para que su hijo/a use los servicios de la biblioteca pública local. Las bibliotecas son magníficos recursos de información social y cultural, y brindan mucho más que libros. A menudo ofrecen relatos de cuentos para niños en los fines de semana donde su hijo/a puede conocer amigos y practicar el inglés en una atmósfera diferente a la del salón de clase. También presentan películas y videos infantiles y a veces tienen talleres especiales de obras manuales para los niños.

NOTA: Si usted u otro miembro de la familia habla inglés, realice las actividades en inglés con su hijo/a. Si no sabe inglés, hágalas en su propio idioma porque de cualquier forma le ayudarán a su hijo/a en su desarrollo socio/cultural y facilitarán su transición al salón de clase estadounidense.

Dear Parents,

Your child is learning English in school, but at the same time he or she is observing different types of social and cultural behaviors. Some of these behaviors may seem confusing or threatening to your child. Be sure to check with your child's teacher if you see any signs of deep unhappiness or anger in your child when he or she talks about school. Make your child's adjustment as smooth as possible by working with his or her teachers.

1. Cultural Sharing. If your child's school does not already have a similar event, suggest a day of cultural exchange in which your child and his or her classmates talk about their family origins, country, and traditions. The children could bring maps, traditional costumes, pictures, photos, music, and foods from their cultures to display and enjoy.

2. Fitting In. Many children worry about "fitting in," being accepted by their classmates and friends. One way you can help your child fit in is by encouraging him or her to get involved in music or sports. Most schools have a band or orchestra or music class where your child can learn to play a musical instrument. All schools have sports teams for boys and for girls; joining a team will provide your child with a new interest and another way to make friends. Be sure to attend any performances or games your child is a part of. Take photos of these events and keep them in a special scrapbook.

3. Right or Wrong. Have frequent talks with your child about different behaviors he or she has observed or heard about concerning classmates. Common issues include smoking, cheating, having a girlfriend or boyfriend, staying out late, sleeping overnight at a friend's house, dress codes, wearing makeup, extreme haircuts, parental rules, and so on. Discuss these issues in a neutral way, both from the point of view of your own culture and from the point of view of the new culture. You can also bring up similar issues using the behavior of people in TV programs and movies.

NOTE: If you or other family members speak English, do the activities in English with your child. If you do not, do them in your own language, and they will still help your child focus on strategies that will eventually transfer to better listening comprehension in English.

Estimados padres de familia:

Su hijo/a está aprendiendo inglés en la escuela, y a la vez está observando distintos tipos de comportamiento social y cultural. Algunos de estos comportamientos pueden confundir o asustar a su hijo/a. Si nota que su hijo/a manifiesta tristeza o rabia al hablar de la escuela, es importante que hable con su maestro/a. Juntos pueden ayudarle a adaptarse.

1. **Intercambio cultural.** Si la escuela de su hijo/a aún no tiene un evento similar, sugiera un día de intercambio cultural en el que su hijo/a y sus compañeros hablen acerca de su origen familiar, su país y sus tradiciones. Los niños pueden llevar mapas, trajes tradicionales, ilustraciones, fotos, música y comidas de sus culturas para exhibir y saborear.

2 **Actividades recreativas.** A muchos niños les preocupa el no ser aceptados por sus compañeros y amigos. Un modo de ayudar a su hijo/a en este sentido es animarlo a que participe en actividades musicales o deportivas. La mayoría de escuelas tienen una banda, orquesta o clase de música donde su hijo/a puede aprender a tocar un instrumento musical. Todas las escuelas tienen equipos deportivos para niños y niñas. El pertenecer a un equipo le dará a su hijo/a un nuevo interés y otro modo de hacer amigos. Asista a cualquier presentación o partido en el que su hijo/a participe. Tome fotos de estos eventos y manténgalos en un álbum especial.

3. **Correcto o incorrecto.** Hable a menudo con su hijo/a acerca de distintos comportamientos de sus compañeros que ha observado o escuchado. Entre los asuntos comunes figuran fumar, hacer trampa, tener novia o novio, llegar tarde a la casa, dormir en la casa de un amigo o amiga, modas, maquillaje, cortes de cabello exagerados, reglas impuestas por los padres, etc. Comente estos temas de modo neutral, tanto desde el punto de vista de su propia cultura como de la nueva cultura. También puede abordar el tema basándose en el comportamiento de personajes de televisión y cine.

NOTA: Si usted u otro miembro de la familia habla inglés, realice las actividades en inglés con su hijo/a. Si no sabe inglés, hágalas en su propio idioma porque de cualquier forma le ayudarán a su hijo/a en su desarrollo socio/cultural y facilitarán su transición al salón de clase estadounidense.

Basic Spelling Vocabulary and Rules

Consonant	Any letter of the English alphabet except for a/e/i/o/u
Stressed	The condition in which a word or part of a word is said more loudly, with more force
Suffix	A letter or letters added to the end of a word to make a new one
Syllable	Each part of a word that contains a single vowel sound
Vowel	Any one of the letters a/e/i/o/u of the English alphabet

1. Write *i* before *e*, except after *c* or when pronounced like *a*.

i before e:	bel**ie**f	n**ie**ce	sh**ie**ld
e before i:	c**ei**ling	rec**ei**ve	w**ei**ght
Exceptions:	either	leisure	neither
	seize	species	weird

2. When a word ends in *y* preceded by a consonant, change the *y* to *i* before every suffix except *-ing*.

cop**y**	cop**ie**s	cop**ying**
fl**y**	fl**ie**s	fl**ying**
worr**y**	worr**ie**d	worr**ying**

3. When a word has only one syllable and ends with a single consonant preceded by a single vowel (such as *fat* or *ship*) and you add a suffix beginning with a vowel, double the final consonant.

dr**ip**	dri**pp**ing	p**op**	po**pp**ing
fl**at**	fla**tt**er	r**ot**	ro**tt**ed
m**ug**	mu**gg**ing	sw**im**	swi**mm**er

4. When a word has more than one syllable and the final syllable (which ends with a single consonant preceded by a single vowel) is stressed and you add a suffix beginning with a vowel, double the final consonant.

admit	admitted	occur	occurring
confer	conferred	submit	submitting

5. When a word ends in a silent *e* and you add a suffix, drop the *e* if the suffix begins with a vowel, but keep the *e* if the suffix begins with a consonant.

desire	desirous	soothe	soothing
like	likable	use	usable
care	careful	move	movement
love	lovely	use	useful

Exceptions:	gentle	gently
	possible	possibly
	simple	simply

6. When a word ends with a silent *e* and you add a suffix, keep the *e* if it is preceded by *c*, *g*, or *s* and the suffix begins with *a*, *o*, or *u*.

close	closure	manage	manageable
courage	courageous	notice	noticeable

7. When a word ends in *ee* and you add a suffix, always keep the final *ee*.

agree	agreeable	flee	fleeing
disagree	disagreeing	see	seeing

The Sounds of English
The Alphabet

Letter	Symbol/Sound	Letter	Symbol/Sound
a	/e/	n	/ɛn/
b	/bi/	o	/o/
c	/si/	p	/pi/
d	/di/	q	/kyu/
e	/i/	r	/ɑr/
f	/ɛf/	s	/ɛs/
g	/ǰi/	t	/ti/
h	/eč/	u	/yu/
i	/ɑɪ/	v	/vi/
j	/ǰe/	w	/'dʌbəl,yu/
k	/ke/	x	/ɛks/
l	/ɛl/	y	/wɑɪ/
m	/ɛm/	z	/zi/

Vowel Sounds

Symbol	Examples	Symbol	Examples
/i/	even, tree	/ə/	away, pencil
/ɪ/	in, did	/ɚ/	murder, Saturday
/e/	April, date	/ɑɪ/	kite, style
/ɛ/	bed, leather	/ɑʊ/	how, shout
/æ/	sad, laugh	/ɔɪ/	boy, voice
/ɑ/	box, father	/ɪr/	beer, fear
/ɔ/	bought, off	/ɛr/	bear, share
/o/	boat, open	/ɑr/	car, park
/ʊ/	book, would	/ɔr/	door, pour
/u/	do, student	/ʊr/	sure, tour
/ʌ/	mother, sun		

85

Consonant Sounds

Symbol	Examples	Symbol	Examples
/p/	map, pack	/z/	always, zip
/b/	back, club	/š/	sugar, vacation
/t/	material, tie	/ʒ/	garage, vision
/d/	dog, mad	/h/	behind, hello
/k/	come, quick	/m/	may, some
/g/	good, dog	/n/	know, fun
/č/	check, nature	/ŋ/	angry, song
/d/	judge, major	/w/	anyone, wet
/f/	fan, laugh	/l/	like, mail
/v/	van, of	/r/	door, red
/θ/	breath, thing	/y/	onion, you
/ð/	breathe, thus	/t/	bottle, mutter
/s/	bus, city	/t/	button, mutton

Common Grammatical Terms

Adjective   A word that describes some quality of a noun or pronoun.

Example: Jimmy has a *new, blue* bicycle.

Adverb   A word that describes or adds to the meaning of a verb, adjective, or other adverb.

Example: Kay shouted *loudly,* but *unfortunately* nobody heard her.

Article   A word used before a noun to show if the noun is a particular or general example of something.

Example: *An* apple *a* day keeps *the* doctor away.

Complement   A word or phrase that follows the verb and describes the person or thing that is the subject of the verb.

Example: The weather is *cold* and *rainy.* You look *depressed.*

Conjunction   A word such as *and* or *but* that connects parts of sentences, phrases, or clauses.

Example: Sally plays basketball *but* her brother plays soccer.

Gerund   A noun formed from the present participle of a verb.

Example: *Swimming* is fun, but I like *skating* more.

Infinitive   The base form of a verb, used with the preposition *to.*

Example: David likes *to play* video games.

Noun   A word that represents a person, place, thing, quality, action, or idea.

Example: The *teacher* lost her *book.*

Object   The person or thing affected by the action of the verb.

Example: Sylvia called *Jack* on the phone. Jerry closed the *window*.

Preposition   A word used in front of a noun, pronoun, or gerund to show place, time, purpose, and so on.

Example: Let's meet *in* Room 5 *at* 4:00 PM *to* do our homework.

Pronoun   A word that substitutes for a noun or a noun phrase.

Example: Today is Mary's birthday; *she* is twelve years old.

Subject   A noun or pronoun that usually comes before the verb in a sentence and refers to the person or thing doing the action.

Example: *Cathy* is studying for a test. The *lights* went out yesterday.

Verb   A word that describes an action, experience, or state.

Example: Jorge *kicked* the winning goal in the soccer game.

Irregular Verb List

Base Form	Simple Past	Past Participle
be: am/is/are	was/were	been
become	became	become
blow	blew	blown
break	broke	broken
bring	brought	brought
build	built	built
buy	bought	bought
catch	caught	caught
choose	chose	chosen
come	came	come
cut	cut	cut
do	did	done
draw	drew	drawn
drink	drank	drunk
eat	ate	eaten
fall	fell	fallen
feel	felt	felt
find	found	found

Irregular Verb List

Base Form	Simple Past	Past Participle
fly	flew	flown
forget	forgot	forgotten
get	got	gotten
give	gave	given
go	went	gone
have: have/has	had	had
hear	heard	heard
hide	hid	hidden
hold	held	held
hurt	hurt	hurt
keep	kept	kept
know	knew	known
leave	left	left
lie	lay	lain
lose	lost	lost
make	made	made
mean	meant	meant
meet	met	met

Irregular Verb List

Base Form	Simple Past	Past Participle
pay	paid	paid
put	put	put
quit	quit	quit
read	read	read
ride	rode	ridden
run	ran	run
say	said	said
see	saw	seen
sell	sold	sold
send	sent	sent
sing	sang	sung
sit	sat	sat
sleep	slept	slept
speak	spoke	spoken
spend	spent	spent
stand	stood	stood
swim	swam	swum
take	took	taken

Irregular Verb List

Base Form	Simple Past	Past Participle
tear	tore	torn
tell	told	told
think	thought	thought
throw	threw	thrown
understand	understood	understood
wake	woke	woken
wear	wore	worn
win	won	won
write	wrote	written